LEGAL PROVISION IN THE RURAL ENVIRONMENT

LEGAL PROVISION IN THE RURAL ENVIRONMENT

Legal Services, Criminal Justice and Welfare Provision in Rural Areas

edited by

CHRISTOPHER HARDING
and
JOHN WILLIAMS

UNIVERSITY OF WALES PRESS
CARDIFF
1994

Published by the University of Wales Press in collaboration with the Centre for Law in Rural Areas, University of Wales, Aberystwyth.

British Library Cataloguing-in-Publication Data.
A catalogue record for this book is available from the British Library.

ISBN 0-7083-1228-4

Cover design by Design Principle, Cardiff
Typeset by The Midlands Book Typesetting Company, Loughborough
Printed in Great Britain by Biddles Ltd., Guildford

Contents

The Contributors

W. J. Edwards is a Lecturer in Geography and co-director of the Rural Surveys Research Unit at the University of Wales, Aberystwyth. His research interests are in rural social geography with particular reference to applied rural research. He has published widely on this theme with an emphasis on community development, housing issues, and the provision of legal and other rural services.

Christopher Harding is a Reader in Law at the University of Wales, Aberystwyth, and teaches in the fields of criminal justice, European law and public international law. He has published a number of books and papers within the general field of criminal justice, the penal system and penal history. These include works on the history of the prison system and theoretical discussion of the nature and purpose of punishment. He has recently been involved in a project which has investigated the impact of European legal developments on the operation of criminal justice.

Pat Hirst was formerly a Tutor, then Lecturer in the Department of Law, at the University of Wales, Aberystwyth. She has been carrying out research in the general area of police studies, and in particular has investigated the impact of legislative changes on the operation of police procedures.

Lynne Hurley graduated in History from the University of Wales, Aberystwyth, and has carried out research into the operation of non-statutory agencies working with ex-offenders. She was for some time a regional organizer in Wales for the National Association for the Care and Resettlement of Offenders.

Margaret Gwynne Lloyd is a magistrate and was also formerly a Research Officer in the Department of Law at the University of Wales, Aberystwyth, and the holder of a Cropwood Fellowship at the University of Cambridge Institute of Criminology. She has researched extensively into the operation of the French prison system and has published a number of papers relating to the methods of dealing with dangerous mentally disordered offenders in the French criminal justice system. She is currently a member of the Mental Health Act Commission.

Paul Robertshaw is a Lecturer at the Cardiff Law School, University of Wales, Cardiff. He has researched extensively into the operation of the legal and criminal justice systems and published widely in the field of public law. A special focus of his research has been the provision of legal services and procedures, as reflected in his recent work on the nature and outcome of criminal court proceedings in England and Wales.

David Rogers is a Lecturer in Geography at Trinity College, Carmarthen. Prior to that he worked in the Rural Surveys Unit at the University of Wales, Aberystwyth. He has a special interest in rural development themes and has undertaken research on the Welsh language and the maintenance of Welsh culture.

John Williams is a Senior Lecturer in Law and Dean of the Faculty of Economic and Social Studies at the University of Wales, Aberystwyth. His main areas of research are social welfare law and health law. He has published a number of books and articles on these topics. Recently he was involved in a research project on the provision of medical services in rural and urban Wales.

1

Introduction: legal services, criminal justice and welfare provision in rural areas

CHRISTOPHER HARDING and JOHN WILLIAMS

As a general subject, the practical working of the legal system – in particular the operation of criminal justice and the issue of access to legal and welfare services – has attracted considerable attention over the last twenty years or more, and there has in this period been a notable development of research studies into the practice of law, especially as it affects that section of the community (in effect, the majority) who are not habitually involved in the legal process. This attempt to establish a view of the legal system 'from below' is associated with a theoretical concern to redress what is increasingly perceived as a one-sided perspective presented by the conventional 'textbook' view of law and the legal system. Traditional accounts of law are, perhaps not surprisingly, written very much by lawyers for lawyers, and the main protagonists in this kind of discussion of law – with the exception of criminal proceedings and, in more recent years, family issues – are the favoured minority with the necessary resources and cultural familiarity to use legal processes in an active way. Even that important category of less favoured individuals who do become significantly engaged in the legal process, criminal defendants, find themselves in that position not out of choice but as the 'passive' objects of legal proceedings. From the 1960s onwards the new socio-legal expertise which has developed as an increasingly important aspect of legal scholarship has been used to address the issue of what law means to the ordinary individual, as distinct from the propertied and commercial parties who have traditionally predominated in the discussion of much substantive law. As a result of this kind of inquiry, often passing under the general label of 'socio-legal' research, much has been brought to light concerning the inadequacies and even injustices of both substantive law and the legal system as they relate to many members of society. In the same way that much history has been reinterpreted by taking the view from below, in particular by emphasizing the social and the informal as distinct from the political and the formal, so too has our understanding of law been subject to such an important revaluation.

However, impressive as this effort of research into the underside of the legal system has been, it has (and in contrast with much of the mould-breaking social history of recent decades) been carried out in a markedly urban context. The point is made in one of the papers which follow, at least in the context of criminal justice research, that this is partly a matter of the researcher's own location (usually a large town or conurbation) and partly a question of the first *obvious* site of study. In quantitative terms, most law takes place in those areas where most people are to be found and where the largest network of social and legal relations is likely to develop. It is an inescapable fact that there are many more lawyers, courts and law enforcement agents in urban than in rural areas. For this reason much socio-legal work has bypassed the rural environment and consequently presented a critical picture of the legal system which has a strongly urban resonance. Yet it would be wrong to assume that a quantitatively less significant range of socio-legal issues in the rural context are also qualitatively less significant or less interesting. Most would surely accept that it would be unduly optimistic to assume that all is well in the countryside simply because it is the countryside; it would be naïve to think that there are no major problems for the legal system or for the implementation of law in its rural context. Moreover, such problems as do exist may not only be worth investigation for the sake of their own solution – the rural legally disadvantaged deserve this no less than their urban counterparts – but also because of their possibly distinctive character, so that lessons of a more general kind may be drawn from the examination of the legal system in a different kind of environment. It is for such reasons that some initial probing into what may be conveniently termed in shorthand fashion 'rural justice' now appears as timely and necessary.

Not surprisingly, the impetus for these research directions has come in particular from institutions and personnel themselves located in the more rural parts of the country. Research into some aspects of law in the rural environment was under way in another 'fringe' of the country at the University of Exeter when the Centre for Law in Rural Areas at Aberystwyth decided to promote the present collection of papers as a kind of prospectus for wider-ranging investigation. But the present volume also has a decidedly Welsh slant and exploits local material and the strongly rural character of much of Wales to investigate the operation of rural law and justice. Although it would be wrong to present the following collection as purely Welsh – indeed some relevant material and much comparative observation has to come from beyond the borders of Wales – there is none the less an important input of original empirical and other relevant material foraged from rural parts of Wales which gives the collection a certain regional flavour. This is a fact that perhaps should not be lost in the final analysis. In the course of the following discussion there is inevitably some reflection on the allocation of resources at a national (i.e. British) level and on the impact of centrally worked out policy on regional problems. Wales is pre-eminently a 'region' (in the European sense – to leave aside for the present arguments about national and ethnic identity) and for that reason also a suitable site for much of the empirical inquiry and observation which is reported in this collection.

Another characteristic of some of the work which is now emerging on law in rural areas is the coming together of two disciplines which have not in the past been especially associated with one another: law (or perhaps, to be more exact, socio-legal study) and human geography. It is no accident that one of the contributions to this collection is by geographers turning their attention towards legal issues, while some of the contributions of socio-legal authorship have inevitably to draw upon some geographical concepts and analysis, particularly as regards the central question of what counts as 'rural' in the context of this kind of research. Indicators of rurality are far from novel to geographers in their own field, but attempts to apply such concepts to socio-legal phenomena such as criminal justice are only just beginning to be made. Similarly, lawyers and researchers in the legal field are becoming more interested in demographic processes as the impact of the latter on the provision of legal services, resourcing the legal system and the development of some substantive areas of law becomes increasingly evident to policy-makers. In this respect the rural environment is no less significant as a site for research studies than urban areas. In recent years demographic changes in many rural districts have accelerated as increasing personal mobility, changing patterns of occupation, residence and leisure, and the development of communications have contributed to changes in the rural way of life. In so far as the papers in this collection suggest the existence of particular problems of rural justice, these are not only, and perhaps not so significantly, problems which arise from the more traditional aspects of the rural environment as complications which have been brought about by demographic change in the later part of the twentieth century.

As already indicated, the broad subject-matter of this collection comprises the general concept of rural justice and welfare provision. This concept suggests in the first place the operation of law through those most visible and dramatic institutions for its implementation, courts of law. Indeed, two of the studies focus upon the provision of justice at two levels of courts, both involved in the provision of criminal proceedings, the magistrates and Crown Courts. But, as with much of the preceding socio-legal research in the urban context, it is imperative to give a good part of the attention to the less visible if more everyday aspects of the legal system. The provision of legal services, and in particular suspected inadequacies in this provision, require discussion and one of the papers addresses this area, dealing with access to legal services. But, as is the case with many attempts to view the legal system from below, much of the space has to be given to that area of justice which has potentially the greatest impact in personal terms on the lives of individuals – that concerned with the criminal process. As well as studies of the working of criminal courts, problems of policing and the role of non-statutory agencies dealing with both offenders and victims form the subject of two other papers. A further paper seeks to provide an overview of research into the criminal justice field and to put these particular studies of rural criminal justice into a broader context. Finally, some of these concerns about the provision of legal services and the kind of social problems which may act as a trigger on the criminal law process come together in the discussion of community care provision, a subject of increasing legal regulation but one which has a distinctive profile in the rural environment.

2

The Provision of Legal Services in Rural Wales

W. J. EDWARDS and D. ROGERS

Introduction

The post-war period has seen an uneven pattern of demographic and socio-economic change in all rural areas in Britain. Many remoter rural regions initially experienced considerable decline and selective out-migration, but since the mid-1970s most of these areas have experienced a resurgence in their population which has reversed decades of decline.[1] As population increases and the age structure of rural communities changes, greater pressures are inevitably placed on some services rather than others. Most attention has been concentrated by rural planners and academics on issues of transport and accessibility, retail servicing, housing, health care and schooling, where declining provision has been characteristic; there is now also apparent a growing concern with access to a range of other professional services.[2] Past concern with service provision in rural areas has concentrated both on physical provision and on the access that different social groups, each operating under varying personal constraints, have for satisfying their needs. The evidence suggests that within most rural populations there are substantial numbers of people who find meeting their needs locally problematic

[1] An examination of the recent changes restructuring the geography of post-war Britain is presented in A. G. Champion and A. R. Townsend, *Contemporary Britain* (London, 1991).

[2] Detailed discussion of the geographical reorganization of services can be found in A. W. Gilg, *An Introduction to Rural Geography* (London, 1985) and in A. G. Champion and C. Watkins (eds.), *People in the Countryside: Studies of Social Change in Rural Britain* (London, 1991).

– the young, the housebound, the poor, the handicapped, the disadvantaged and the elderly – and in many rural areas these problems are intensifying.

Rural populations, however, are not unchanging; demographic and economic restructuring has occurred in even the remoter rural areas. Retirement and return migration by older people and the repopulation of the countryside by younger families have reshaped towns and villages, bringing both new skills and services and some new needs and expectations in terms of the provision of services to rural areas. Consequently, different patterns of service are demanded and a wider range of professional skills are now present in the countryside. This is not to argue that access to such services is comparable for all residents, but rather to suggest that patterns of demand for and supply of such services have changed considerably.

This is as true of the service provided by the legal profession as it is of the village bus, local shop or school, but far less is known of changes in the first than the others. Consequently, this chapter explores three themes. Initially, to provide a context, consideration is given to the issue of access to legal services and how this topic has been approached in both American and British studies. Secondly, attention is concentrated on work dealing with access to justice in rural Britain and the findings that have emerged over the last few years from work undertaken in Exeter. Finally, the provision and background of solicitors practising in rural areas of Wales is examined in order to explore both how provision has changed and to establish the current structure of the profession.

Recognition of the Problem

Within the wider field of access to justice, there has been considerable discussion of the provision of legal services. This has been concerned with provision, access and need, and with the general agreement that a large section of the public is denied the legal advice and assistance it requires.[3] The existence of this unmet legal need, along with a general feeling that not enough was known about legal services, their organization and efficiency, led to the setting up of two Royal Commissions on Legal Services,

[3] B. Abel-Smith, M. Zander and R. Brooke *Legal Problems and the Citizen* (London, 1973), ix; P. Morris, 'A sociological approach to research in legal services', in P. Morris, R. White and P. Lewis, *Social Needs and Legal Action* (London, 1973), 47-72, at 48; M. Zander, *Legal Services for the Community* (London, 1978), 273; M. Blacksell, K. Economides and C. Watkins, 'Legal services in rural Britain: access, accessibility and need', 'Access to Justice in Rural Britain Project', AJRBP working paper 2 (Exeter, 1984), 5.

the reports of which have been the subject of considerable debate.[4] In particular, attention has been drawn to the varying definitions of legal services as given in the reports. The report for England, Wales and Northern Ireland (the Benson Report) was criticized for restricting the provision of legal services to lawyers, and disregarding the legal work of lay persons and advisory groups associated with housing, welfare and consumer affairs.[5] On the other hand, the report for Scotland (the Hughes Report) has been praised for its more visionary stance, seeing legal services as 'advice, information or assistance involving a knowledge of rights and obligations conferred by law and of legal procedures, whether provided by a lawyer or otherwise . . . whether the client is an individual, a group or an organisation'.[6] These reports suggest, although there is some difference in interpretation between them, that legal provision might be expanded to a multiple system with professional, lay and other services combining to improve access to legal information.

Further problems arise when the concept of need for such services is addressed. The Lord Chancellor's Legal Aid Committee, in evidence given to the Royal Commission, stated that they did not believe there was an exact degree of unmet need measurable by scientific inquiry,[7] and that need is a relative concept involving a judgement of some kind.[8] Such a definition provides minimal encouragement to those who might seek an unequivocal statement of latent demand for legal services. This study cannot address this important question of need and is, instead, primarily concerned with the legal services provided by solicitors. None the less, it does recognize the necessity for further inquiries into local residents' needs and the important role played by other agencies in meeting such needs, through the provision of both legal and quasi-legal advice to rural residents.

Pioneer enquiries into both patterns of provision and access to

[4] *Report of the Royal Commission on Legal Services*, Cmnd 7648 (1979); *Report of the Royal Commission on Legal Services in Scotland*, Cmnd 7846 (1980); for a discussion of both reports see A. Paterson, 'Legal services for all', *Journal of Social Welfare Law* (1980), 321–9, and LAG (Legal Action Group), *Legal Services, a New Start: LAG's Response to the Report of the Royal Commission on Legal Services* (London, 1980).

[5] Paterson, op. cit. (1980), 321; LAG, op. cit., 5.

[6] Paterson, op. cit. (1980), 321.

[7] Zander, op. cit. (1978), 276.

[8] Morris, op. cit. (1973), 50–3; Zander, op. cit. (1978), 273–6; Abel-Smith *et al.*, op. cit. (1973), 109; for a discussion on the concept of social need and how it can be measured see J. Bradshaw, 'The concept of social need', *Ekistics*, 220 (1974), 184–7.

legal services were undertaken in America. Carlin and Howard summarized a number of questionnaire studies undertaken from the 1940s onwards, which were mainly directed at the urban poor.[9] Various factors were identified as being involved in the unequal use of lawyers. Lack of economic resources was only one element in a complex social process which also included the awareness or recognition of the problem as legal, willingness to take legal action, getting to a lawyer and actually hiring a lawyer.[10] Mayhew and Reiss, in a survey of legal problems and experiences in Detroit, used fourteen types of legal problems, similar to those applied in a later study by Abel-Smith *et al.*, and analysed these with reference to characteristics such as age, sex, race, income, social status, education and home ownership.[11] These studies, with their strong urban emphasis, provide some general indication of factors that might be considered in any analysis of legal services and such studies have also been undertaken in Britain.

Most of the early research on legal services in Britain has been concerned with the geographical distribution of solicitors. These studies have explored the relationship between provision and population, underlying which has been the concept of 'territorial justice', that is that available resources should be distributed in accordance with need.[12] In particular, Abel-Smith and Stevens calculated the number of persons per solicitor in counties, county boroughs and urban districts with a population of 30,000 or over. They drew attention to the considerable nationwide variation, from under 850 persons/solicitor in places such as Bournemouth, Brighton and Guildford to over 10,000 persons/solicitor in Salford and over 24,000 persons/solicitor in Wallsend.[13] A similar approach was adopted by Zander who used the 1967 Law List, supplemented by personal inquiry, to show that for urban London, 69 per cent of solicitors' firms were located in 5 per cent of the postal districts.[14]

A more comprehensive London-based study by Abel-Smith, Zander and Brooke actually emphasized at the outset that the choice of study area was one of pure convenience rather than one arising from a belief that unmet need was greater in urban areas

[9] J. E. Carlin and J. Howard 'Legal representation and class justice', in V. Aubert (ed.), *Sociology of Law* (Harmondsworth, 1969), 332–50.

[10] Aubert, *Sociology of Law*, 343.

[11] L. Mayhew and A. J. Reiss, 'The social organization of legal contacts', *American Sociological Review*, 34 (1960), 309–18, at 313.

[12] K. Foster, 'The location of solicitors', *Modern Law Review*, 36 (1973), 153–66, at 153.

[13] B. Abel-Smith and R. Stevens, *In Search of Justice* (London, 1968), 152.

[14] M. Zander, *Lawyers and the Public Interest* (London, 1968), 212.

than in more sparsely populated areas.[15] As well as describing the legal and advisory services available in the boroughs of Islington, Southwark and Tower Hamlets, the study included a questionnaire administered to 1,700 members of the public drawn from the electoral register, enquiring whether they had been in any of seventeen specific situations which required legal advice in the previous seven years, and if so, what action and advice had been taken. Respondents were asked questions to establish their knowledge of the legal and advisory services available. Their attitudes to the legal system were also examined.[16]

The geographical distribution of solicitors in England and Wales was also studied by Foster who used the 1971 Law List as his basic source. Of particular interest in that study was the reference to solicitors' offices, rather than individual solicitors. Foster assumed that the existence of a solicitors' office was more important to an individual with a legal problem than the actual number of solicitors.[17] In his study, Foster also attempted to compare the distribution of solicitors with that of other professionals such as doctors and dentists and to test whether the distribution of legal services was related to five key socio-economic indicators in towns with a population of over 50,000.[18]

Since Foster's work, other relevant studies in the British context include a study by Bridges *et al.* of legal services in Birmingham and one by Glasser which involved a statistical analysis of referral lists of solicitors undertaking legal aid work in 1975.[19] A study by Podmore of the West Midlands Metropolitan County area also investigated the role of solicitors in the community with reference to their involvement in local organizations and politics.[20] Far less

[15] Abel-Smith, Zander and Brooke, op. cit. (1973), x.

[16] Ibid., xiii, 114–15.

[17] Foster, op. cit. (1973), 154.

[18] Ibid., 158–9; the socio-economic indicators used were: (i) % of population in social classes I and II, (ii) % of owner-occupied households, (iii) % of population 65+, (iv) a commuting ratio (comparing residents and non-residents in employment in the area and elsewhere), (v) retail sales per head. The strongest correlation produced was that between the distribution of solicitors and the amount of retail sales per head.

[19] L. Bridges, B. Sufrin, J. Whetton and R. White, *Legal Services in Birmingham* (Birmingham, 1975); C. Glasser, *The Distribution of Solicitors' Offices undertaking Legal Aid Work*, unpublished report (1977) presented to Royal Commission on Legal Services; both cited in C. Watkins, M. Blacksell and K. Economides, 'The distribution of solicitors in England and Wales', *Transactions of the Institute of British Geographers*, NS, 13 (1988), 39–56, at 55–6.

[20] D. Podmore, *Solicitors and the Wider Community* (London, 1980), cited in M. Blacksell, K. Economides and C. Watkins, 'Country solicitors: their professional role in rural Britain', *Sociologia Ruralis*, 27 (1987), 181–96, at 183.

has been known, except in general terms, about the provision of legal services in rural areas, but this has recently been rectified by a major project undertaken at Exeter.[21]

Legal Provision in Rural Areas

The obsessive concern with the delivery of legal services in urban areas has been described simply as 'inner-city infatuation',[22] and there is, in consequence, a need to explore the rural dimension of legal service provision.[23] This is seen by Watkins *et al.* as 'a significant omission which ought to be rectified',[24] especially in the light of the otherwise extensive geographical literature on rural service provision. Indeed, even the Royal Commissions did not examine in detail the problems facing rural areas; the Benson Report, for example, noted from its survey of 8,000 individuals that people living in rural areas were more likely to consult solicitors than their urban or suburban counterparts, and that one possible way of maintaining or extending a certain level of service would be the provision of interest-free or low-interest loans for solicitors in rural areas.[25] The Hughes Report, however, did draw attention to the particular severity of unmet need in the rural areas of Scotland,[26] adding that certain measures were required to bring legal advice services to remote rural communities.[27] In general, the response of both Royal Commissions to the particular needs of rural areas was seen to be disappointing. Without doubt, the most important study dealing with the rural provision of legal services in the UK has been the 'Access to Justice in Rural Britain Project' (AJRBP) based at the University of Exeter, the findings of which were issued as a series of working papers from October 1984 to December 1986. Recently, these have been published in a text dealing with access to justice in rural areas.[28] Access to legal services is discussed, with

[21] M. Blacksell, K. Economides and C. Watkins, *Justice outside the City: Access to Legal Services in Rural Areas* (London, 1991).

[22] K. Economides, 'Legal services and rural deprivation', *Bracton Law Journal* (1982), 41.

[23] M. Blacksell, A. Clark, K. Economides and C. Watkins, 'Legal services in rural areas: problems of access and local need', *Progress in Human Geography*, 12, 1 (1988), 47–65, at 60.

[24] Watkins, Blacksell and Economides, op. cit. (1988), 39–56.

[25] Blacksell *et al.*, op. cit. (1987), 182.

[26] LAG, op. cit. (1980), 48.

[27] Blacksell *et al.*, op. cit. (1987), 182. The increased awareness by the Hughes Report of the problems of rural areas is probably due to the evidence given by bodies such as the Highlands and Islands Development Board (HIDB), Crofters' Commission and the Western Isles Council.

[28] Blacksell, Economides and Watkins, op. cit. (1991).

emphasis on the fact that accessibility is concerned with matters other than physical distance.[29] In particular, reference is made to economic, geographical and psychological barriers which inhibit the use of legal services.[30] Economic constraints are seen to consist of either a universal limitation imposed by poverty, that is, inability to pay, or a realization that the return gained from following a claim would not be worth the effort.[31] Geographic constraints refer to the distance from the point of supply, with the argument that those living in rural areas suffer disproportionately compared with urban dwellers; while psychological barriers may include lack of legal knowledge or legal competence, due possibly to the limited provision of educational or advice and information services, as well as local and or cultural constraints.[32]

Central to the AJRBP was a detailed study of solicitors and access to legal services in Devon and Cornwall, focusing upon the solicitors themselves, solicitors' firms, the types of work undertaken and access by clients.[33] In addition, a number of regional reports were commissioned so that findings from the Devon and Cornwall study could be related to findings made elsewhere. Such regional reports were prepared for rural Norfolk, rural Scotland and rural Dyfed, although much of the fieldwork involved took place at a much more local level.[34] A report was also commissioned to describe the provision of public legal services to rural areas in the United States.[35]

The Devon and Cornwall study involved the survey of a total of eighty-three solicitors, thirty-two from rural Devon, twenty-nine from Cornwall and twenty-two from the more urbanized areas of Exeter, Plymouth and Torbay.[36] Results from the survey showed that solicitors' firms in rural areas were more likely to be

[29] Blacksell *et al.*, op. cit. (1984), 10.

[30] E. Johnson, in vol. 3 of the Florence Access to Justice Project (1979), 3–168; cited in Blacksell *et al.*, op. cit. (1984), 10.

[31] Blacksell *et al.*, op. cit. (1984), 10.

[32] Ibid., 11–12; see also M. Slatter and M. Moseley, 'M'rural friend', *New Law Journal*, 136 (1986), 626–8, 641.

[33] M. Blacksell, K. Economides and C. Watkins, 'Solicitors and access to legal services in rural areas: evidence from Devon and Cornwall', AJRBP working paper 6 (Exeter, 1986), 3.

[34] M. Slatter and M. Moseley, 'Access to legal services in rural Norfolk', AJRBP working paper 7 (Exeter, 1986); A. Paterson and S. Bain, 'Access to legal services in rural Scotland', AJRBP working paper 13 (Exeter, 1986); P. Thomas, 'Access to legal services in rural Dyfed, Wales', AJRBP working paper 11 (Exeter, 1986).

[35] C. Britt, 'The delivery of public legal services to rural areas: the American experience', AJRBP working paper 5 (Exeter, 1986).

[36] Blacksell *et al.*, op. cit. (1986), 2.

partnerships, with fewer sole principals and assistant solicitors than in urban areas. They are also more likely to provide a generalist service as opposed to specialization in any particular area of law.[37] It was suggested that remote, sparsely populated areas could be unattractive to new entrants (calculated from the date when articles were taken), and both earnings and opportunities were perceived as being lower.[38] The survey also highlighted the unprecedented number of firms founded during the last decade, although some dissatisfaction was voiced regarding branch offices and peripatetic legal surgeries in terms of cost and organization, with solicitors commenting that the public were mobile enough.[39] Some wariness was also expressed about the introduction of information technology such as word processors, computer accounting and computer time-costing, with a fear that such developments might depersonalize solicitor/client relations.[40] Types of work undertaken by solicitors revealed the overwhelming importance of residential conveyancing, in terms of both income and time, followed some way behind by wills and trusts, family and general litigation.[41] However, 78.3 per cent of firms did take on work which they knew to be unprofitable, although some categories of work were not taken on.[42] In general, practices in rural areas were seen as being less competitive than those in urban areas, but solicitors saw little fundamental differences between rural and urban firms and almost 82 per cent thought that legal services in rural areas were adequate.[43]

Two further studies were undertaken in Devon and Cornwall; a survey of the twenty-four Citizens' Advice Bureaux (CABx) organizers[44] and a study of the use of legal services by 355 respondents in three remote rural parishes.[45] Although solicitors themselves in rural areas tended to feel that legal services in rural areas were adequate, over half the CABx organizers did not share the same view, and supported proposals for establishing mobile CABx and community resource lawyers.[46] Of the groups consulting a solicitor most frequently, farmers, business and professional

[37] Ibid., 3–4.
[38] Ibid., 4 and 7.
[39] Ibid., 9–11.
[40] Ibid., 15–16.
[41] Ibid., 18–19.
[42] Ibid., 22.
[43] Ibid., 25 and table 46 on p. 29 of Appendix.
[44] Thomas, op. cit. (1986), 11–20.
[45] C. Watkins, M. Blacksell and K. Economides, 'The role of CAB in rural areas', AJRBP working paper 12 (Exeter, 1986b).
[46] C. Watkins, M. Blacksell and K. Economides, 'The use of legal services in three remote rural parishes', AJRBP working paper 14 (Exeter 1986c).

categories each ranked highly, and the telephone was seen as the most important means of first contacting a solicitor.[47] Only a very small proportion (5 per cent) of respondents had consulted the legal services of a trade union or professional body. Overall, respondents were reasonably satisfied with the provision of legal services, although problems mentioned included quality of service, lack of public transport, lack of publicity and lack of advice.[48]

The second of the regional reports commissioned by the AJRBP was that prepared by Paterson and Bain for rural Scotland with particular reference to East Ross. Interestingly enough, an earlier survey for the Hughes Report found that 61 per cent of Scottish respondents had never consulted a solicitor as opposed to 41 per cent of English respondents.[49] Similar results to the Devon and Cornwall study were found regarding the generalist nature of rural practices with a shortage of solicitors specializing in child law, consumer law and welfare and housing law.[50] Reference was also made to the non-rural nature of the CABx network.[51] The rural Scotland study also described two experiments in generalist advice provision which are worthy of mention.

During the late 1970s, the Scottish Consumer Council, working under the Highland Regional Council, set up an experimental 'freephone' service for north-west Scotland, administered by Inverness CABx.[52] This advice-line scheme, covering approximately 2,200 square miles, continues to this day but suffers from insufficient publicity, which is seen as crucial for such a service to be successful.[53] However, the attractiveness of the scheme is its efficiency and reliability, and this has led to the setting up of three other advice-line schemes in Aviemore and Grantown on Spey, Ross and Cromarty and Shetland.[54] In addition to advice-lines, the Scottish Consumer Council has been involved with a number of 'Village Link' schemes, where workers and volunteers operate from their own homes in villages throughout the area. The first Village Link scheme, set up in 1978 in the Grampian region, was not a success and was discontinued in 1981.[55] A village scheme

[47] Watkins *et al.*, op. cit. (1986b), 41.

[48] Watkins *et al.*, op. cit. (1986c), 8.

[49] Ibid., 20–1; for a review of the quality of lawyer's services as seen by clients, see M. Zander, *The State of Knowledge about the English Legal Profession* (Chichester, 1980), 55–7.

[50] Paterson and Bain, op. cit. (1986), 10.

[51] Ibid., 12.

[52] Ibid., 15.

[53] Ibid., 17.

[54] Ibid.

[55] Ibid., 18.

for the Galloway area has proved to be more successful by using fewer links but aiming for a higher degree of public exposure.[56] Another project, involving the appointment of a welfare rights officer and jointly funded by the Scottish Association of CABx and the Highland Region, was initiated in 1985 but was regarded as being too recent to evaluate in terms of success.[57] An earlier study of consumer problems in rural Scotland by Mackay and Laing, although finding very little dissatisfaction among respondents regarding legal services,[58] made several recommendations relevant to lawyers in rural areas, namely that peripatetic services should be developed to improve access by rural consumers and that the use of community buildings such as schools should be experimented with. It was also found that official forms and applications were a particular problem.[59] Finally, Mackay and Laing stressed that Gaelic speakers might have particular language difficulties.[60]

Two further surveys were also commissioned for Norfolk and Dyfed based on small samples of solicitors. The regional report for rural Norfolk centred on a case study of the North Walsham area, which involved interviews with five solicitors and eight local contacts, as well as an appraisal of some local initiatives involving the delivery of legal services to rural areas. Included among these initiatives were an ultimately unsuccessful attempt at establishing a law centre for Norwich and Norfolk, the Norfolk Rural Advice and Information Project (NRAIP) established in 1984, jointly funded by the Development Commission and three town councils, and also the work of a resourceful and progressive solicitor in private practice.[61] Of particular interest in the Norfolk report is a comprehensive list of factors which stress the importance of a free and accessible legal advice service in rural areas, compiled by the co-ordinator of NRAIP.[62]

The second of these small surveys dealt with access to legal services in rural Dyfed, with particular reference to the town of Haverfordwest.[63] Interviews were conducted with eight solicitors, one from each of the town's seven practices, and one from Crundale, a village located a few miles to the north-east of Haverfordwest. The traditional nature of the firms was emphasized, with the majority of work covering conveyancing, wills, probate and trusts. Certain

[56] Ibid., 19.
[57] Ibid., 20.
[58] G. A. Mackay and G. Laing, *Consumer Problems in Rural Areas* (Edinburgh, 1982).
[59] Ibid., 139.
[60] Ibid.
[61] Slatter and Moseley, op. cit. (1986), 22.
[62] Ibid., 23.
[63] Thomas, op. cit. (1986).

categories of work were regarded as uneconomic because of the small size of firms, which limited the range of services provided by each practice. One unique feature, stressed in the Dyfed report, was that 'within the UK it is only in Wales that language might be perceived by indigenous people as a barrier to legal services.'[64] This is reinforced by various CABx reports which show that under stress people will always wish to use their mother tongue, which will be Welsh for a considerable proportion of rural Dyfed's population.[65] In Dyfed, legal services will be sought by both English and Welsh speakers; provision therefore needs to be bilingual if appropriate service is to be provided.[66] As in the Devon and Cornwall study, there was agreement among solicitors that legal services in rural areas were adequate, indeed all solicitors in the Haverfordwest sample agreed that this was the case.[67] A study of access to legal services and CABx in south Wales by D. Beale and B. Stow stresses the point, however, that deprivation of specialist legal help is a particularly rural problem, and also points out that elderly villagers are often reluctant to ask for advice and help because of their traditional passivity and the lack of privacy present in many small rural communities.[68] Discussion of alternative sources of legal advice, other than that provided by solicitors in private practice, is limited in the Welsh study to the work of the only law centre in Wales in Adamsdown, Cardiff; the South Wales Anti-Poverty Action Centre (SWAPAC), which was discontinued in 1981; a West Glamorgan Law Project, proposed but lacking funding, and the role of the CABx.[69]

This brief review of the literature suggests a general concern with uneven patterns of professional legal provision. Although much work has focused on urban areas, more recent research has demonstrated a rural dimension to the problem, which has not always been recognized by solicitors in private practice. Clearly, the growing interest in both the form of current provision and the ways in which such provision can be made more accessible is an arena worthy of further inquiry. While the latter might be an appropriate focus for research, studies in the former area are far from comprehensive, and more still needs to be established about the current profile of provision in rural regions. The Exeter study

64 Ibid., 5.

65 *CAB News* (Spring 1985), 5, cited in Thomas, op. cit. (1986).

66 Thomas, op. cit. (1986), 26.

67 Ibid., 27.

68 Cited in Thomas, op. cit. (1986), 16; the particular problems facing the elderly are also noted in Slatter and Moseley, op. cit. (1986a), 628.

69 Ibid., 11–15.

has successfully delineated the key issues, but some of their regional case studies were highly localized and place-specific. Therefore the final section of this chapter seeks to add to their findings by exploring the provision of professional legal services delivered by solicitors throughout rural Wales. Particular attention in this subsequent discussion is given to the way the legal profession has responded to the changing demand for services which has arisen because of population growth and economic restructuring since the 1970s.

Legal Provision in Rural Wales

A variety of possible frameworks exists for formally defining the extent of rural Wales. These range from those using purely administrative boundaries to more academic, regional definitions based on relatively sophisticated multivariate analysis. For convenience, this study has adopted the definition of 'extreme rural areas' provided by Cloke and Edwards.[70] Their multivariate classification based on a range of demographic, housing, occupational and mobility indicators suggests, as figure 2.1 shows, that most of Dyfed (with the exception of Llanelli), all of Gwynedd and Powys, and two districts in Clwyd can be viewed as 'extreme rural areas'.

This classification however is based on administrative district data, and legal services are not provided on a district basis; rather they are provided through offices based in the major urban centres. Inevitably people living on the edges of these areas defined as rural will look to the nearest town for the provision of legal services. This may well mean that, on the southern and eastern boundaries of the study area, they draw on services lying outside the rural heartland, simply because towns there are more accessible. For practical purposes, in the analysis that follows, only law practices based in towns where their hinterland or travel-to-work area lies wholly within the rural area are included in the discussion. Few solicitors in rural Wales are located in villages outside the main towns, and these towns themselves are small in size. It is therefore inappropriate to draw the distinction made in the Devon and Cornwall study (AJRBP) between urban and rural practices.

Within this bounded area, contemporary population trends are in marked contrast to those of the past. Since the nineteenth century, this region has experienced substantial depopulation, but this trend has now been reversed. Between 1971 and 1981 only one district recorded a slight decrease in population; the remainder showed varying degrees of growth. A decrease of 0.9 per cent was

[70] P. J. Cloke and G. Edwards, 'Rurality in England and Wales 1981: a replication of the 1971 index', *Regional Studies*, 20, No. 4 (1986), 289–306.

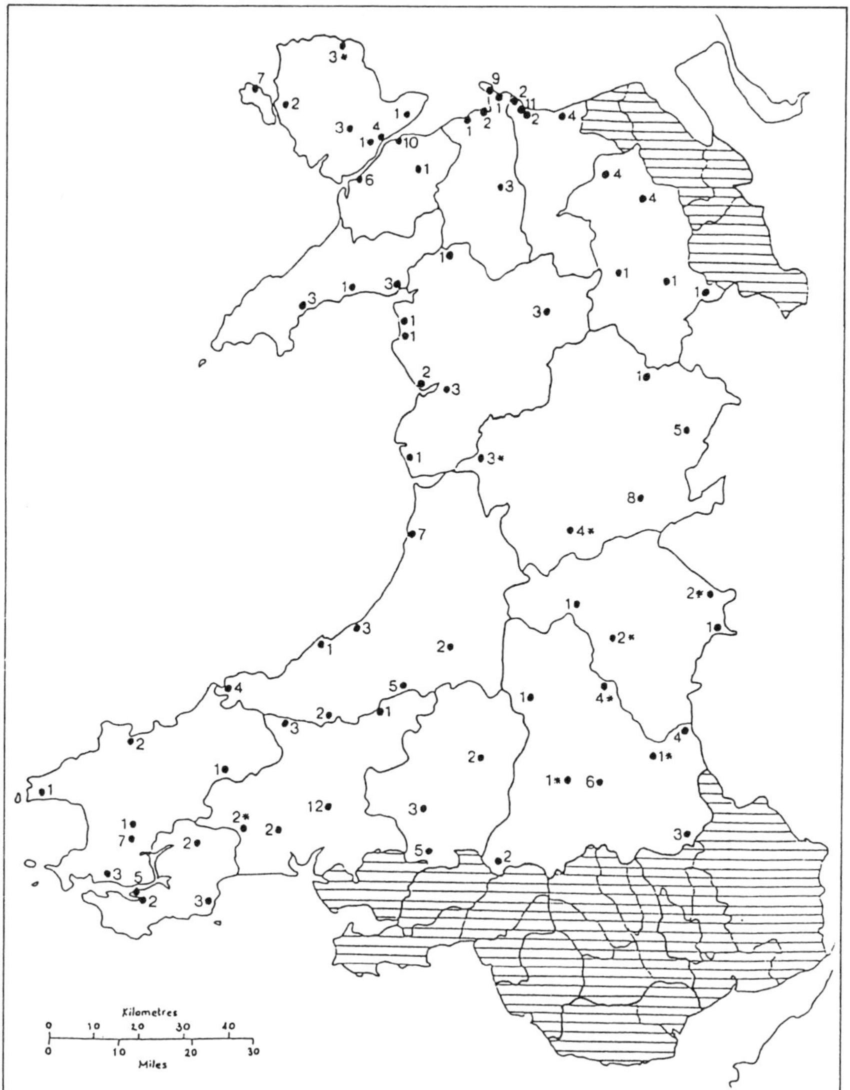

KEY

●1 Total number of offices

●3* One office has restricted opening

Districts not designated as 'extreme rural' (Cloke's 1981B index)

Within rural Wales:
Total of 187 firms
236 offices (10 part-time)
379 practising solicitors

Figure 2.1 *Distribution of solicitors' offices in rural Wales*

Table 2.1 *Population change in rural Wales*

	Population 1981 ('000s)	Population 1989 ('000s)	% Change 1981–5	% Change 1985–9	Migration 1981–9 ('000s)	Migration 1981–9 % 1989 population
Colwyn	49.1	56.2	2.8	11.2	9.7	17.2
Glyndŵr	40.3	42.4	−0.5	5.6	2.8	6.6
Carmarthen	51.9	56.7	3.3	5.7	5.7	10.1
Ceredigion	61.2	69.0	1.0	7.2	8.8	12.8
Dinefwr	37.2	39.0	−0.2	5.0	2.8	7.2
Preseli	69.2	70.2	1.6	−0.2	0.2	0.3
S. Pembs.	38.3	43.0	1.7	10.3	4.5	10.5
Aberconwy	51.3	54.3	1.8	3.9	5.2	9.1
Arfon	54.6	56.0	−1.0	3.6	0.8	1.4
Dwyfor	25.9	27.6	1.6	4.7	2.7	10.4
Meirionnydd	31.4	32.1	0.1	2.1	1.5	4.7
Anglesey	68.0	70.9	2.4	1.7	1.9	2.7
Brecknock	40.9	41.4	0.4	0.7	1.1	2.7
Montgomery	48.4	52.1	1.1	6.5	3.9	7.5
Radnor	21.3	23.3	0.8	8.6	2.4	10.3

Source: OPCS Monitor PP1 90/1 1990, table 4, p. 16
Note: Net migration* = in-migration − out-migration

recorded in Arfon, but most other local authorities experienced a population increase between 5 and 10 per cent. Radnor experienced a particularly significant increase of 17.7 per cent. In only five districts was natural increase a contributor to growth; in all other areas net migration accounted for the advances in population totals.

Since 1981, these trends have continued. As table 2.1 reveals, the mid-year population estimates from the Office of Population Censuses and Surveys (OPCS) indicate continuing rates of population growth in most areas between 1981 and 1989. Rates of increase in excess of 5 per cent have occurred in Colwyn, South Pembrokeshire, Radnor, Ceredigion, Montgomery and Dinefwr, and only in Preseli did population decline slightly from 1985 to 1989. What is noticeable is that in many areas a significant contribution to this growth is a result of net migration rates during the period 1981–9. This is most marked in Colwyn and Aberconwy in the north, Ceredigion, Carmarthen and South Pembrokeshire in the west and Radnor in the east of Wales. These trends are confirmed by evidence on annual migration from the National Health Service Central Register (NHSCR) for the same period. This evidence gives some indication of the rates at which population in rural Wales is being restructured, as retirement and other forms of migration have an impact on particular localities. These changes provide opportunities for the legal profession in rural Wales, whether it be through involvement in house conveyancing, the establishment of businesses, through the growth of crime, or through the wide range of possible legal requirements of households both young and old. It is therefore pertinent to speculate on how the legal profession, assessed through the distribution of solicitors, has responded to such demographic changes.

The Relationship between Population and Provision

The Law List, published from 1775 to 1976, and more recently the *Solicitors' and Barristers' Directory* have both been used as a data source for a number of studies concerned with the distribution of solicitors. Since 1984 the *Directory* has contained additional information regarding the location of solicitors and the categories of work undertaken by them.

The *Directory* contains an entry for every solicitors' office in the country, as well as names of individual solicitors in those offices. The Law Society also encourages solicitors to give information regarding their status within the firm, qualifications, date of admission as a solicitor and the categories of work which firms and individual solicitors undertake. Firms and individual solicitors are indexed alphabetically as well as being listed by town.

Two main sources of error, identified by Watkins *et al.*[71] in their analysis of the 1985 *Directory*, apply in using these data. Firstly, there is the possibility of double-counting solicitors, as they may appear under the entry of more than one town if a certain firm has a number of branch offices. In addition there is also the problem of non-return of information and incomplete information being supplied by solicitors. Both types of error will be referred to as they arise in the analysis of the *Directory*.

Foster used this source in his analysis of the location of solicitors in 1971, as did Watkins *et al.* in their study of solicitors in England and Wales in 1985.[72] This chapter also uses the *Solicitors' Regional Directory for Wales* in 1988 to construct a profile of the legal profession in rural Wales, by examining the entries for solicitors' firms, offices and individual solicitors themselves.[73] Because of the problems of error noted above, it was decided that

[71] Watkins *et al.*, op. cit. (1988).
[72] Foster, op. cit. (1973); Watkins *et al.*, op. cit. (1988).
[73] Law Society, *The Solicitors' Regional Directory (Wales)* (London, 1988).

Table 2.2 *Number of persons per solicitor in rural Wales, 1971–1988*

	% Pop. change 1971–88	% Change in solicitors 1971–88	No. of solicitors		Persons per solicitor	
			1971	1988	1971	1988
Cardigan	22.1	21.0	38	46	1438	1457
Caernarfon	11.9	32.8	58	77	2117	1770
Montgomery	18.7	35.0	20	27	2138	1896
Radnor	23.6	0.0	7	7	2609	3229
*Carmarthen	*	*	*60	*42	*2705	*2255
*Brecon	*	*	*17	*28	*3131	*1468
*Denbigh	*	*	*71	*51	*2603	*1888
Meirionnydd	−11.4	63.6	11	18	3207	1756
Pembrokeshire	13.8	74.2	31	54	3475	2085
Anglesey	18.8	81.3	16	29	3717	2448

Sources: Foster (1973); *Solicitors' Directory Wales* (1988); OPCS 1971, 1981, 1990.
*Comparisons inappropriate because of boundary differences

the most accurate method of obtaining the number of solicitors was to use the index of individual solicitors provided by the *Directory*. Although this method seems to avoid the danger of double-counting individual solicitors, it is likely that the estimate obtained is somewhat conservative as a result of the incomplete nature of the information provided by a number of solicitors. This material does allow a fuller examination of the provision in rural Wales than that provided by the study of solicitors in the Haverfordwest area of Dyfed, which is not necessarily typical of the whole of rural Wales.[74] Before exploring the 1988 evidence, it is useful to discuss the pattern of provision that the previous studies identified; by so doing, the responsiveness of the legal profession to demographic change can be specified.

Unfortunately administrative divisions changed considerably as a result of local government reorganization between 1971 and 1981, and this limits longer-term comparative analysis. Foster's work was based on the traditional county divisions of England and Wales in 1971, and many changed significantly after 1974. Table 2.2 reassembles the data for those countries where reasonable comparisons can be drawn between 1971 and 1988/9. In three cases such comparisons are inappropriate because the data for 1971 and 1988 are not for the same areas or populations. However, for the

[74] Thomas, op. cit. (1986).

Table 2.3 *Potential clients/persons per office and solicitor by district in rural Wales in 1988/9*

District	Persons per office	Persons per solicitor	Percentage population growth (1981–9)
Ceredigion	2792	1457	12.7
Brecknock	1868	1468	1.2
Dwyfor	3000	1500	6.6
Glyndŵr	3458	1729	5.2
Carmarthen	2790	1744	9.2
Aberconwy	3381	1745	5.8
Meirionnydd	2633	1756	2.2
Montgomery	2560	1896	7.6
South Pembs.	3223	1905	12.3
Arfon	2905	1971	2.6
Colwyn	3044	2030	14.5
Preseli	4713	2209	1.5
Anglesey	3550	2448	4.4
Radnor	3767	3229	9.4
Dinefwr	3890	3890	4.8

Sources: *Solicitors' Directory* (1988); OPCS Mid Year Population Estimates, 1990.

remaining old traditional counties it is clear, with one exception, that the number of solicitors has increased at a comparable rate to, or faster than, the total population. This has led to lower numbers of population per solicitor, and, it could be argued, better territorial service. Surprisingly this has not been the case in the old county of Radnor, a district where population increased rapidly during this period. This may well be a result of the fact that solicitors are available in nearby towns outside the county, for example in Newtown, Shrewsbury, Hereford and other smaller towns. Watkins *et al.* noted comparable changes throughout England and Wales for the 1971–85 period, with a dramatic growth in the number of solicitors, so that the median number of persons per solicitor fell from 3,041 in 1971 to 1,911 in 1985.[75] In 1971, five Welsh rural districts fell below the median figure for that year, and in 1985 only three had higher ratios than the median value. The major improvement in access that lower numbers of people per solicitor might imply appears to have operated over these years in both countries. It is worth noting, however, that, against a general trend

[75] Watkins *et al.*, op. cit. (1988).

of improvement in ratios within rural Wales, some differences exist between districts.

By 1988, Ceredigion, Brecon and Dwyfor had the most favourable relationship with the lowest number of people per solicitor (1,500 or less). Arfon, Aberconwy, Glyndŵr, Meirionnydd, Montgomeryshire, Carmarthen and South Pembrokeshire had between 1,501 and 2,000 per solicitor. Preseli, Colwyn and Anglesey had between 2,000 and 3,000, and Radnor and Dinefwr over 3,000 per solicitor (table 2.3). If these groupings are compared with the situation in 1985, then it is apparent in many areas that the recruitment of additional solicitors has not matched the rise in population from 1985 to 1989, and in many districts the number of persons per solicitor has shown an increase. This is most marked in Radnor, Dinefwr, Colwyn, Anglesey and Preseli. This classification suggests that the heartland of Welsh-speaking rural Wales is generally adequately served. Around this core, the periphery shows varying levels of service, with particularly poor provision in selected districts where population is increasing rapidly. Such intra-regional variation suggests that it is appropriate to explore more closely the local variation in supply of services.

Figure 2.1 and table 2.4, based on evidence from the *Solicitors' Directory* (1988), show the distribution of solicitors in rural Wales. They indicate that there were 187 solicitors' firms and 236 solicitors' offices in rural Wales in 1988, of which ten had limited opening hours, and a total of 379 solicitors.[76] Solicitors are concentrated in the main settlements of each district with individual urban centres recording between one and twelve offices. The greatest recorded concentrations of offices are in Carmarthen (twelve), Colwyn Bay (eleven) and Bangor (ten), but many other main district centres have more than five firms.

The districts differ in the geographical concentration of practices. Foster quite correctly emphasized the importance of the number of offices (see tables 2.3 and 2.4), as well as the proportion of population per solicitor.[77] The relative concentration or dispersion of offices is a critical factor in determining access. In some districts firms are found in as many as seven centres, while in others only three towns offer solicitors' services. The relative location of these towns also affects accessibility from other parts of the district – in Colwyn and Aberconwy, offices are concentrated on the north Wales coastal belt, and this is in marked contrast to the distribution in other areas where firms are dispersed more regularly

[76] Tregaron does not appear in the index as having a solicitors' office. However, the entries of two Lampeter firms reveal that there are offices at Tregaron.

[77] Foster, op. cit. (1973).

Table 2.4 *Number of offices and solicitors, rural Wales, 1988*

	Offices		Total solicitors(S)		Female solicitors(F)		
	no.	%	no.	%	no.	F%S	%
Ceredigion	24	8.5	46	12.1	9	19.6	10.2
Carmarthen	20	8.5	32	8.4	4	12.5	8.5
Preseli	15	6.3	32	8.4	5	15.6	6.3
Aberconwy	16	6.8	31	8.2	8	25.8	6.8
Anglesey	20	8.5	29	7.6	6	20.7	8.5
Arfon	19	8.1	28	7.6	3	10.7	8.1
Brecknock	22	9.3	28	7.6	4	14.3	9.3
Colwyn	18	7.6	27	7.1	4	14.8	7.6
Montgomery	20	8.5	27	7.1	4	14.8	8.5
Glyndŵr	12	5.1	24	6.3	4	16.6	5.1
South Pembs.	13	5.5	22	5.8	4	18.2	5.5
Meirionnydd	12	5.1	18	4.7	2	11.1	5.1
Dwyfor	9	3.8	18	4.7	1	5.5	3.8
Dinefwr	10	4.2	10	2.6	2	20.0	4.2
Radnor	6	2.5	7	1.8	0	0.0	0.0
Total	236	100.0	379	100.0	60	–	100.0

Source: *Solicitors' Directory* (1988)

throughout the district. Such patterns reflect the main concentration of population and the local urban systems, but they inevitably mean that for a minority of people in remote locations access to such services can be achieved only by correspondingly greater effort. In rural Wales, access is further complicated by geography and the limited provision of appropriately timetabled public transport services. These complications are particularly intractable for the non-car-owning and elderly population.[78]

The *Directory* not only provides evidence of the geographical location of provision, but also a considerable amount of information about the solicitors who are practising in the various firms. It has been noted by Blacksell *et al.* that, in addition to the attractions of living and working in rural areas, the high status accorded to rural solicitors in both the community and the work setting acts as an added incentive, compensating for financial disadvantage, to keep

[78] Moyes, A., *The Need for Public Transport in Mid-Wales: Normative Approaches and their Implications*, Rural Surveys Research Unit Monograph 2, Department of Geography (Aberystwyth, 1989).

the number of solicitors in the countryside high.[79] A measure of status in the workplace is provided by the *Directory*, which records that 282 (74.4 per cent) are partners, 71 (18.7 per cent) assistant solicitors and twenty-six (6.9 per cent) consultants. The 'partners' category could be subdivided further, with eighty-two solicitors (29.1 per cent) of the 282 concerned being listed as the only partner of that firm. However, to claim that all of these are sole principals would be unwise because of the incomplete nature of some of the returns. These figures are based on the individual solicitors' index to avoid double-counting, but they do suggest that the opportunities available in many rural firms are likely to be attractive to newly qualified practitioners.

Rural law appears, from the evidence in the *Directory* to be predominantly a male profession. Only sixty (15.8 per cent) of the solicitors practising in rural Wales in 1988 were women. This is an improvement on the data for England and Wales presented by the Royal Commission on Legal Services (Benson Report, 1979) where only 6.5 per cent were women, and it is clear that more women are finding employment in rural districts.[80] Closer examination of the distribution of female solicitors reveals that the three districts of Ceredigion, Anglesey and Aberconwy account for over 38 per cent of all female solicitors. The districts of Dwyfor, Meirionnydd and Dinefwr have only five women solicitors between them, while Radnor has none at all.

Particularly pertinent to the theme developed earlier, of the legal profession as a service responding to demand from an increasing population in rural Wales, is the evidence the *Directory* provides of the date of admission as a solicitor. Table 2.5 reveals that a large

Table 2.5 *Dates of admission of solicitors practising in rural Wales in 1988*

	Total	%	Male	%	Female	%
1921–30	2	0.5	2	0.6	0	0.0
1931–40	8	2.1	8	2.5	0	0.0
1941–50	27	7.1	27	8.5	0	0.0
1951–60	46	12.1	41	12.8	5	8.3
1961–70	68	17.9	65	20.4	3	5.0
1971–80	146	38.5	119	37.3	27	45.0
1981–7	82	21.6	57	17.9	25	41.7
	379	100.0	319	100.0	60	100.0

Source: *Solicitors' Directory* (1988)

[79] Blacksell *et al.*, op. cit. (1991).
[80] Cited in Blacksell *et al.*, op. cit. (1986), p. 1 of Tables.

number of solicitors were admitted in the 1971–80 period, and this period marks the onset of more widespread female recruitment, with 87 per cent of women solicitors admitted after 1970. Total recruitment was high in 1970, dropped slightly in the four years that followed, and then, during the last years of the 1970s, showed a consistently high annual increase reaching a peak in 1980, when twenty-seven of those now practising were admitted. Throughout the 1980s the annual total pattern of admission has progressively fallen to only seven in 1987. On average, five women have entered solicitors' firms every year since 1974, and as a proportion of new entrants they have increased every year throughout the 1980s. This level of recruitment is at odds with the conclusions in the Devon and Cornwall study, which suggested that remoter rural areas were less attractive to new entrants to the profession.[81]

Examination of the patterns of admission for each district reveals some interesting contrasts. All solicitors who qualified prior to the 1940s are male and are in practice in seven western and north-western districts. They are found in four districts of Gwynedd – Aberconwy, Arfon, Dwyfor and Meirionnydd – and three in Dyfed – Carmarthen, Ceredigion and South Pembrokeshire. In most districts, except Radnorshire, recruitment was low but steady during the 1950s and 1960s. Radnorshire is unusual in that nearly 60 per cent of solicitors in the district were admitted to the profession in the 1960s. Most districts peaked in terms of admissions after 1970. This was most evident in Montgomeryshire, where 77.8 per cent of solicitors were admitted after that date, no doubt in part reflecting the development of Newtown and the rapid growth of population in the area. Other rural districts show around 60 per cent of new admissions after 1970, with most arriving before 1981, again reflecting overall population trends. Dinefwr and Ceredigion are distinctive in experiencing far fewer new admissions in these years, and in both cases less than 50 per cent of those practising arrived after 1970. Such variation in the length of experience of solicitors practising in rural Wales may in part reflect job satisfaction and stability, and in part the necessity for growth to meet increasing demand. Whatever the reason, it is likely to have an influence on the character, experience and attitudes of those practising in the legal service in particular localities.

It is difficult to establish the origins and prior experience of solicitors who are now working in rural Wales, as this information is not collected by the *Solicitors' Directory*. This is of interest because

[81] M. Blacksell, K. Economides and C. Watkins, 'Solicitors and access to legal services in rural areas: evidence from Devon and Cornwall', AJRBP working paper 6 (Exeter, 1986).

it is often suggested that an increasing number of the professional people working in these rural areas have few or no local Welsh ties. Some evidence on this theme emerges from a recent examination of the demand for continuing education in rural Wales, where over a quarter of the solicitors currently practising provided some relevant information on this topic.[82] The questionnaire used in that survey provided some interesting information about the background of the respondents and their employment experience prior to taking up their current position. The data collected suggests that many of the solicitors who are currently practising in rural Wales do have established ties with these areas, and most have considerable experience in Wales.

Of the 105 solicitors who provided information in the survey, nearly 60 per cent provided information on where they obtained their qualifications. Over half of these graduated through the University of Wales, with the remainder obtaining initial qualifications in a number of English universities including Oxford, Cambridge, London, Liverpool and Bristol. These respondents were very similar to the total population described earlier, with 9.5 per cent qualifying during the 1950s, 10.5 per cent in the 1960s, and high proportions (40.9 and 39 per cent respectively) in the 1970s and 1980s. Thirteen (12.4 per cent) of the respondents were women, which again is similar to the proportion recorded in the *Solicitors' Directory*.

Information was also obtained from ninety-two solicitors on previous employment. Of these, nearly 40 per cent were still in the first employment they obtained in rural Wales immediately after qualification. Of the remaining fifty-six solicitors, over half (thirty) had only one other appointment prior to their current one and, in all but seven cases, this had been in Wales. These Welsh appointments were mainly in the rural districts, but seven solicitors in this group had worked in urban centres in south Wales. Ten solicitors had held two positions previous to their current employment; in four cases these were again both in Wales; in a further four, they had involved both English and Welsh offices, while in only two cases had this experience been wholly in England. A further nine solicitors had worked in three or four different locations; in all these cases most of the offices had been in Wales. Seven other respondents indicated that they had worked in various employments but provided no details of where these had been based. Most solicitors had been engaged in private practice, with less than 10 per cent of appointments being with local authorities and the public sector.

[82] W. J. Edwards and D. Rogers, *An Investigation into the Demand for Continuing Education in Legal Matters in Rural Wales*, Final Report of PICKUP LAW/RSRU project, Rural Surveys Research Unit, UCW (Aberystwyth, 1989).

The collective record of this sample suggests that many solicitors in rural Wales are Welsh in origin. No doubt in some areas language proficiency encourages this localism, but these data suggest that many of the legal profession in rural Wales have trained, or gained experience and first appointments, in rural offices and chosen, in many cases, to remain in rural Wales for the course of their professional lives. Consequently, any rise in level of provision to meet the demand from increasing rural populations during the 1970s and 1980s has provided professional opportunities in Wales for many who, if demographic trends had been different, might have only found employment further afield in urban centres in England.

It has been suggested by Blacksell *et al.* that income distribution, employment, the age structure and character of populations, all generate considerable demand for legal services, which has encouraged the expansion of provision in rural areas.[83] Certainly many of these factors have contributed to the rising provision of such services in these Welsh districts. Although there is considerable discussion about lower levels of income in rural Wales, levels of saving are known to be high and the characteristic income distribution is bi-modal. Change in farming during the 1970s and 1980s has seen considerable farm amalgamation and the sale of smaller, less viable units. The predominantly elderly population, ranging from 18.8 to over 30 per cent in many districts, increases the likelihood of will and probate specialisms and contributes subsequently to house conveyancing. Retirement and younger adult in-migration has led to population growth and all incomers require housing.

The combination of high proportions of elderly in the population and high proportions of households occupying new properties is particularly marked in the districts of Colwyn, Ceredigion, South Pembrokeshire and Anglesey. All of these are districts where the provision of solicitors has increased substantially during the 1970s and 1980s. However, these districts are not alone in experiencing such trends. The Welsh housing statistics for 1989 record exceptionally high levels of owner occupation in rural Wales in all districts: in most areas a figure in excess of 80 per cent is characteristic. These levels of ownership generate considerable new business, a point clearly supported by data recorded in the Welsh Intercensal Survey of 1986, which reveals that in most of the rural districts of Wales between 30 and 42 per cent have occupied their property for less than five years. This inevitably generates considerable work in residential conveyancing.

[83] Blacksell *et al.*, op. cit. (1991).

This is borne out by recorded work that is undertaken by solicitors' offices. The *Solicitors' Directory* has, since 1984, included information detailing the categories of work undertaken by solicitors. These categories of work are classified under twenty 'main', and a further eighteen 'other', headings.

In 1988, detailed information regarding categories of work was given by 180 offices (76.3 per cent). Incomplete information was given by 54 offices (22.9 per cent). Table 2.6 illustrates the main categories of work carried out by solicitors, with residential conveyancing, wills and trusts and family law being undertaken by over 90 per cent of all offices. Twenty per cent or less of offices are not involved in housing, agricultural property, general litigation, general and motoring crime and accident litigations. Two-thirds of offices deal with a range of legal problems covering consumer

Table 2.6 *Main categories of work undertaken in legal practice and by solicitors in rural Wales.*

Rank	Category	% offices	% solicitors' involved in work	% solicitors' ranking such work important
1	Residential conveyancing	96.7	82.7	81.6
1	Wills and trusts	96.7	74.3	63.0
3	Family	90.0	74.3	63.0
4	Housing, etc	86.7	64.1	40.1
4	Agricultural property	86.7	62.0	68.0
6	Litigation, general	86.1	59.1	52.0
7	Crime, general and motoring	85.0	62.8	77.5
8	Litigation, accidents etc	82.8	59.1	46.4
9	Consumer problems	77.2	43.5	35.7
10	Commercial property	73.9	42.2	67.0
11	Crime, juvenile	70.6	39.7	48.8
12	Employment	65.0	34.6	18.3
13	Taxation	64.4	24.9	42.3
14	Planning, etc	63.9	28.7	25.0
15	Child care and wardship	63.3	29.1	60.9
16	Business affairs	58.1	42.6	63.4
17	Litigation, commercial	51.1	13.1	22.5
18	Welfare benefits	47.8	8.4	20.0
18	Bankruptcy and insolvency	47.8	16.8	57.5
20	Accident advice	12.2	no data	no data

Source: *Solicitors' Directory* (1988)

Table 2.7 *Other categories of work undertaken in solicitors' offices*

Rank	Category	Offices involved no.	Offices involved (%)	% solicitors involved
1	Liquor, betting and gaming licensing	61	(25.8)	27.8
2	Building contracts	40	(16.9)	15.2
3	Defamation	38	(16.1)	8.9
4	Mental health	29	(12.3)	9.7
5	Charity law	27	(11.4)	8.9
6	Road haulage licensing	26	(11.0)	4.2
7	Insurance law	25	(10.6)	7.6
8	Immigration and nationality	23	(9.1)	3.8
9	Rating law	21	(8.9)	2.5
10	Copyright, patents, designs and trademarks	19	(8.1)	2.5
11	Housing association law	17	(7.2)	3.0
12	Race and sex discrimination	13	(5.5)	0.8
13	Entertainment, artists and performers	12	(5.7)	0.4
13	Pension schemes	12	(5.0)	1.3
15	Mines and mineral law	8	(3.3)	0.8
16	Banking law	7	(2.9)	2.1
17	European human rights	6	(2.5)	1.3
18	Admiralty	5	(2.1)	0.8

Source: *Solicitors' Directory* (1988)

problems, commercial property, juvenile crime, employment, taxation planning law, and childcare and wardship. Less than half of offices deal with welfare benefits, bankruptcies and accident advice. Considerably less than a quarter of offices are involved in the other categories of work listed in table 2.7. These range from sixty-one offices involving themselves with liquor and betting and gaming licensing to five offices experienced in Admiralty law. These variations mean that, inevitably, access to certain legal skills varies somewhat from one part of rural Wales to another. These general findings match those reported in the AJRBP for Devon and Cornwall and rural Scotland.[84]

The relative importance of these different activities in the work of individual solicitors within offices is also specified in table 2.6, and it is clear from this that the type of work described above has had a critical effect in structuring work schedules in individual practices.

[84] Ibid.

Two-thirds of practising solicitors (237) provided data on the most and least important aspects of their individual workloads. There are clear differences in both the number and proportion of solicitors who undertake work in certain categories of law. Of these 237 solicitors, 219 (92.4 per cent) stated that they undertook legal aid cases, although only 87 solicitors (36.7 per cent) were willing to take on emergency cases, and no individual solicitors stated a willingness to conduct a fixed fee interview. However, the proportion of offices recorded as willing to undertake emergency cases and fixed fee interviews was considerably higher.

More than 60 per cent of solicitors are involved in residential conveyancing, wills and trusts, family, housing, criminal and agricultural property law and litigation. Less than half of solicitors are involved with the other categories specified, and under a quarter with some of them. It is also evident that there is a close correlation between areas of law that are widely practised and the proportion of solicitors who evaluate those areas of law as important in their individual workload. It is clear from examination of both tables that there are small numbers of solicitors working throughout rural Wales with a range of specialist legal knowledge, but the majority of work most solicitors undertake falls very obviously into a few major legal categories.

Two points need to be emphasized about the accuracy of information relating to individual solicitors and firms. Firstly, since the information was supplied by the individual solicitors and their offices, there is obviously a degree of bias due to self-reporting, with some solicitors and firms claiming expertise in all categories, while returns for others are obviously incomplete. A further source of error is that many individual solicitors, instead of ranking categories according to the volume of work involved, merely listed them. This was apparent in the returns of a fifth of individual solicitors.

Variations in the categories of work offered by firms in each district, as well as provision of legal aid, fixed fee interview and emergency action can also be established from the *Solicitors' Directory*. In 1988 some firms, in most districts, did not provide a comprehensive response. Consequently, the evidence presented for the twenty major categories of work in table 2.8 is incomplete for some firms in all districts except Dwyfor. These data suggest, that as the client's need moves towards more specialist requirements, the likelihood of obtaining such advice at the nearest office varies from one district to the next.

Table 2.8 provides a summary of the number of firms in every ten in each district which offer a service to clients on each of the twenty main categories of work identified in the *Directory*. The most

Table 2.8 *Categories of work undertaken by offices in the districts of rural Wales*

Rank	Category	% of offices	Districts (number of offices in every ten offering service) 1	2	3	4	5	6	7	8	9	10	11	12	13	14	15
1	Conveyancing	96.7	9	10	10	9	10	9	10	8	10	9	10	10	10	9	10
2	Wills and trusts	96.7	10	10	9	9	10	9	10	9	10	10	10	10	10	10	10
3	Family	90.0	9	10	9	9	10	7	9	6	8	10	9	9	10	10	10
4	Housing, etc	86.7	10	9	9	9	10	9	8	6	8	8	8	9	10	10	9
4	Agric. property	86.7	7	10	8	9	10	9	10	9	9	9	5	9	9	9	9
6	Litigation, general	86.1	10	10	8	9	10	8	8	8	7	8	9	9	10	10	10
7	Crime/general motoring	85.0	9	10	8	9	5	8	8	8	8	10	8	9	9	9	9
8	Litigation, accidents	82.8	9	8	9	8	8	7	8	6	8	9	7	9	9	9	10
9	Consumer problems	77.2	9	8	8	8	5	8	7	5	8	8	5	7	9	10	5
10	Commercial property	73.9	9	9	7	8	5	9	7	4	8	8	7	7	4	8	5
11	Crime, juvenile	70.6	9	6	4	7	5	7	7	5	8	8	6	9	7	7	8
12	Employment	65.0	8	6	6	8	10	9	4	1	6	7	5	6	5	8	9
13	Taxation	64.4	5	6	7	8	8	6	7	5	7	5	5	8	6	6	7
14	Planning etc	63.9	6	6	6	6	5	7	6	3	8	7	5	5	9	9	9
15	Child care	63.3	6	6	6	8	5	7	6	5	7	7	5	6	6	6	8
16	Business affairs	58.1	9	10	8	7	5	8	8	6	9	9	5	8	5	7	6
17	Litigation, commercial	51.1	9	6	6	8	8	5	4	3	6	7	3	5	4	2	5
18	Welfare benefits	47.8	7	6	3	6	5	3	4	3	5	4	5	6	6	6	8
19	Bankruptcy	47.8	5	8	4	7	5	6	4	1	5	6	3	5	4	3	6
20	Accident advice	12.2	-	1	1	1	-	1	1	3	2	1	3	2	–	1	3

Key to Districts: 1=Colwyn; 2=Glyndŵr; 3=Brecknock; 4=Montgomery; 5=Radnor; 6=Carmarthen; 7=Ceredigion; 8=Dinefwr; 9=Preseli; 10=South Pembrokeshire; 11=Aberconwy; 12=Arfon; 13=Dwyfor; 14=Meirionnydd; 15=Anglesey

Source: *Solicitors' Directory* (1988)

important categories of work are covered by more than seven out of ten offices in most districts, but as the categories become more specialized many districts offer them in less than half their offices, and there are noticeable variations between districts for some of these categories of law. Given the geographical variations in both the number and location of offices in many districts, differences in work undertaken by particular practices mean that the public may find it harder to obtain appropriate advice in some areas compared with others. This is particularly true for the sensitive legal services – childcare and wardship, bankruptcy and welfare benefit, and accident advice – which are not provided by all offices in any districts.

For those in greatest need, over 86 per cent of practices administered legal aid, and a fixed fee interview was offered by over 75 per cent of offices. Just over 66 per cent of solicitors' offices offered to undertake emergency cases, but again there is considerable variation between districts in the proportion of firms offering such services. Legal aid is offered by all offices in South Pembrokeshire, Dwyfor, Brecknock and Radnor, but only by 80 per cent of practices in Dinefwr. The fixed fee interview is offered by all practices in Radnor but by less than 70 per cent in Carmarthen. In Dinefwr only half the firms deal with emergency action, and in most other areas only six out of ten firms handle such cases.

This suggests that for some rural residents, often those in greatest need, getting appropriate advice in rural areas is not always easy. Nor can the urban-based network of Citizens' Advice Bureaux necessarily provide an accessible alternative to meet the needs of rural residents. The constraints of a limited number of bureaux and extension offices with fixed hours of opening limit access. Rising demand for CABx advice throughout the 1980s suggests that the advisory welfare services are under considerable pressure in trying to meet a demand that is not being fully satisfied through the more usual, conventional legal channels.

Concluding Comments

This chapter has explored one aspect of the growing interest in geographical variation in service provision in rural areas. It has highlighted the rising concern with methods of delivery and the difficulties found in some areas in providing adequate access to legal services. In reviewing the pattern of provision in rural Wales for 1988, it has illustrated the way the legal profession has responded to the demographic change that has taken place since the 1970s. The recruitment of solicitors, their prior experience and their dates of entry into the profession have also been documented, expanding on the findings commissioned by AJRBP for rural Dyfed. While the evidence suggests some improvement in professional service, the geography of provision may pose problems for less mobile clients. This problem is compounded by the variations in categories of law dealt with by solicitors' offices, which means that for some clients, the nearest office may not provide the particular legal specialism they require.

In delineating these geographical and structural characteristics of provision, little more than a skeleton is presented, which requires flesh and substance. More needs to be known about the way individual firms operate; the precise level of demand for particular legal advice; the local requirements for legal services in Welsh; whether some firms provide a more individualized and mobile service to clients, and how they see their professional expertise reaching a broader clientele in the future.

Work also needs to be undertaken on levels of 'hidden need', currently satisfied in part by CABx, but perhaps not drawing on the skills of solicitors in practice because of the economic or psychological barriers that Blacksell *et al.* identify. These findings beg this central question, in that much of the growth in provision has capitalized on the needs of those who represent 'comfortable' Britain, rather than those who are in need of much more advice, guidance and support. This study, however, does provide a context for subsequent work to explore the important question of how effective the current level of legal provision is in meeting the expressed and latent needs of populations in remote rural regions.

3

Research into Criminal Justice in Rural Areas

CHRISTOPHER HARDING

The general impression of crime (and therefore of the operation of criminal justice) in western industrialized societies is that of a predominantly urban phenomenon. This is largely a reflection of the undeniable fact that, quantitatively speaking, most crime occurs in urban areas, which are the main centres of population and have social conditions which are generally seen as being more likely to result in offending behaviour. Such factors as urban social deprivation, interethnic tensions and the urban location of centres of entertainment add to the raw fact of population distribution in generating a view of crime as 'crime in the city'. So we customarily talk of 'street gangs' and 'street violence' and fictional media portrayals of crime and crime control are set typically in such places as New York, Los Angeles, Miami, London and Paris. However, it may be asked whether this is a fair representation of the incidence and significance of criminal activity and of the problems faced by the criminal justice system. A number of the chapters in this book inquire into different aspects of 'rural' criminal justice with a view to identifying any distinctive features and problems encountered in that context. But some preliminary issues in this discussion should first of all be given attention, not least the definitional problem of what constitutes 'rural' and the social significance of 'rural' criminality.

There are some fairly clear reasons why research into the working of the criminal justice system in the UK has its focus on what may be loosely described as urban areas. One crucial factor in empirical studies has been the amount of criminal activity, or perhaps more accurately, criminal justice process, in urban compared to rural areas. Research samples in rural areas may simply be too small to allow for any generalization or conclusion, as Robertshaw notes in his chapter in relation to two of the Crown Courts in his sample.[1] All other things being equal, there is clearly less crime in a purely quantitative sense in rural areas in the UK since there is a much smaller population. (This is true of Britain; it is not necessarily so for other countries with a proportionately larger rural population or, at least, less population concentrated in large cities or conurbations.) It follows that there is likely to be much less in the way of law enforcement and legal processing of offenders. However, the basic issue of quantum may distract attention from some possibly instructive lines of inquiry. For instance, in so far as crime does occur in rural areas, how serious is it in terms of generally accepted scales of criminality?[2] Or are there certain types of offending which are distinctively 'rural' or more likely to occur in rural areas? Or again does the rural environment enable more crime to remain hidden,[3] so leading us into a false sense of the relative incidence of crime as between town and country? Conan Doyle's celebrated detective was confident about this possibility:

> 'Do you know, Watson,' said he, 'that it is one of the curses of a mind with a turn like mine that I must look at everything with reference to my own special subject. You look at these scattered houses, and you are impressed by their beauty. I look at them and the only thought which comes to me is a feeling of their isolation, and of the impunity with which crime may be committed there.'
>
> 'Good heavens!' I cried. 'Who would associate crime with these dear old homesteads?'
>
> 'They always fill me with a certain horror. It is my belief, Watson, founded upon my experience, that the lowest and vilest alleys in London do not present a more dreadful record of sin than does the smiling and beautiful country-side.'[4]

A first cautionary note, therefore, is that we should be careful about figures which are at first sight unimpressive because of their paucity. That fact alone begs questions which deserve at least the benefit of some further inquiry.

[1] See below, p. 52.

[2] Two kinds of question may be posed: (1) Is there *proportionately* more or less 'serious' crime (e.g. crime of violence) in rural than in urban areas? (2) Are certain offences *viewed* more or less seriously in rural than in urban areas?

[3] Once again, this begs a number of further questions, e.g. undetected? unreported? not prosecuted?

[4] Sir Arthur Conan Doyle, 'The Copper Beeches' from *The Complete Short Stories* (London, 1928; 1976 impression), 285–6.

Another factor which has led to a research focus on crime in the city and the suburbs is mundane and pragmatic – the fact that most researchers and their resources are located in urban areas. Those research institutions interested in crime problems (unlike research institutions in other areas such as science and agriculture, many of which are for a number of reasons located in rural areas) are generally situated in large towns or conurbations and will naturally tend to explore their local environment in testing hypotheses concerning the working of the criminal justice system. So, to list just a few examples of research which has been local to the researcher's base: Baldwin and McConville (1977) (base: Institute of Judicial Administration, University of Birmingham; sample: Birmingham Crown Court); Doherty and East (1985) (base: Polytechnic of Wales, Pontypridd; sample: Cardiff Magistrates' Court); Walsh (1980) (base: University of Exeter; sample: Exeter); Zander (1979) (base: London School of Economics; sample: London Crown Courts). For some research the researchers obviously do have to go further afield, particularly if controls are needed for a particular sample. None the less, in practice this often results in other urban centres being chosen. So Vennard (1982), wishing to study contested trials in magistrates' courts, chose samples from six courts: three in London, and three in provincial towns in the north, the west and the Midlands. Baldwin (1985), in his study of pre-trial review in magistrates' courts, for more specific reasons examined practice in courts in Nottingham and Leeds.

It would be misleading to suggest that rural areas tend to be generally ignored in criminal justice research. A good deal of research relates to wide geographical areas, such as Police Authority areas, or court circuits, and necessarily includes a mix of urban and rural. But such research, while it may throw up comparisons between largely rural and largely urban areas, rarely sets out specifically to inquire into the nature of crime and criminal justice in the rural environment. In other words, much of what we know about crime and criminal justice in a rural context has been produced incidentally as part of research studies with other or more wide-ranging objectives.

Some aspects of criminal justice do not easily lend themselves to being categorized as 'urban' or 'rural'. This is perhaps most strikingly so in relation to the use of custodial measures. Most interest in and concern about the use of imprisonment and related types of custody fixes upon the internal operation of these very self-contained institutions, rather than their geographical location. None the less, the latter aspect of custodial institutions has sometimes attracted a certain amount of commentary, for instance in relation to the difficulty of visiting prisoners in more rural locations.[5] Indeed, the location of prisons has recently emerged as a significant concern in the Woolf Report into the Strangeways prison disturbances of 1990, with its proposal for 'community prisons', which would allow prisoners to be kept in custody as near as possible to their homes.[6] And, at a theoretical level, the development of the open Borstal system in the earlier part of this century was partly inspired by the perceived practical advantages of training young offenders in citizenship in rurally located institutions;[7] while on the other hand there have been persuasive reasons for locating maximum security prisons in more sparsely populated areas (typified by the Mountbatten Report's proposal for 'Vectis', a single maximum security prison on the Isle of Wight).[8]

In the final analysis, it is difficult to escape the conclusion that, for a mixture of theoretical and practical reasons, crime and criminal justice in the rural environment have attracted relatively little attention in an otherwise very active field of research. The main question then is whether this is a significant omission, especially in terms of understanding criminal behaviour and identifying the problems of the criminal justice system. The chapters which follow (4 to 7) attempt to answer that question with reference to particular aspects of criminal law enforcement and criminal justice. There is also the question of whether it is possible to identify a distinctively 'rural' criminality, which will be considered later in this chapter. Firstly it is necessary to turn to the underlying definitional and conceptual issue of how 'rural' and 'urban' can be distinguished in this context.

The Concept of a Rural Area

Since few researchers in the criminal justice field have directed their attention specifically to the question of crime and criminal justice in the rural environment, it is not surprising to find little discussion of the problem of identifying what is understood by 'rural'. At the extreme end of the spectrum it is easy enough:

[5] See Mike Fitzgerald and Joe Sim, *British Prisons* (2nd edn., 1982), 72–4. As early as 1927 William Morris had made a gift of £10,000 to make it possible for poor parents to visit their sons in rurally located open borstals (Roger Hood, *Borstal Reassessed* (London, 1965), 117).

[6] *Prison Disturbances 1990: Report of an Inquiry by the Rt. Hon. Lord Justice Woolf and his Honour Judge Stephen Tumim*, Cm 1456 (London, 1991), Part 11.

[7] Hood, *Borstal Reassessed*, 114–20; Victor Bailey, *Delinquency and Citizenship* (Oxford, 1987), 227–40.

[8] *Report of the Inquiry into Prison Escapes and Security (Mountbatten Report)*, Cmnd 3175 (London, 1966).

inner London is as indubitably urban as the Scottish Highlands are rural. In between there is a large geographical area of uncertain description, compounded by rapid social and economic change in some districts. For instance, in his chapter Robertshaw notes the impending ruralization (in some senses, at any rate) of Merthyr Tydfil.[9] Or, then, consider the problem of categorizing a district such as south-west Surrey. In terms of landscape, most of this area would be surely described by many people as rural. Yet in socio-economic terms it may be fairly described as part of 'commuterdom', in that a significant part of its population and their lifestyle is dependent upon and influenced by the metropolis. Landscape and population by themselves are not help helpful indicators,[10] and clearly other criteria must be developed to differentiate the rural from the urban. The point is made clearly by Cloke: 'the terms "urban" and "rural" are used habitually, yet the criteria employed in their definition have often been of a vague and intuitive nature' (1977, 31).

As a starting-point, it may be suggested that the method of classification should depend largely on the nature of the inquiry. In the field of criminal justice, research is concerned principally with patterns of social behaviour, the economic context of the latter and with legal and institutional responses. Given those concerns, it may be argued that population is *one* relevant factor in constructing the criteria of rural character, whereas aesthetic appreciation of the landscape (although important for instance in the context of the visual image of the rural and the urban) is likely to be of only marginal significance. However, even within the general field of criminal justice research, categorization may depend on the more specific field of inquiry. If, for example, research is concerned with the incidence of criminality or crime patterns, the relevant criteria of rural and urban environment may well be seen to include residential distribution, occupational patterns and centres of social activity. It could be argued then, for instance, that a scattered residential pattern, a significant proportion of the population engaged in agriculture with few major centres of social and commercial activity would emphatically indicate a rural environment in terms of patterns of social behaviour. On the other hand, if research is concerned with enforcement of criminal law and the operation of legal procedures, the above criteria may not be so obviously relevant in describing the environment as urban or rural.

[9] See below, p. 52.

[10] 'The way in which society is organised is more important for understanding the prevailing legal culture, than the superficial aspect of the landscape' (Blacksell *et al.* 1991, 19).

In such a context it may be more meaningful to categorize in terms of the distribution of resources, ease of communications and level of contacts between personnel. An area may be rural in terms of population and of social and economic activity, yet if it is endowed with a high level of administrative resources, well-trained personnel and good communications its otherwise rural character may not be a relevant consideration in assessing the operation of the criminal justice process. In fact, research which has specifically focused on aspects of rural criminal justice, such as Henshaw (1988), G. Jones (1990) and P. Hirst in this volume, has stressed elements like resource levels and communications as significant criteria of effectiveness as regards the working of the system. To seek a global test of rurality may therefore not be the most useful approach, and it may be more advantageous to recognize at the outset that there are shifting senses of 'rural', depending very much on the kind of questions asked.

That point made, it may still be helpful to draw upon some of the typologies of geographical areas that have been worked out for other purposes. It may be useful to recall in the first place that there is a well-established local government practice of classifying districts into broadly urban and rural. The former organization of local government in England and Wales, from the end of the nineteenth century through to the early 1970s, made use of a major distinction between urban and rural in dividing many areas into urban and rural districts. The criteria employed for this purpose included factors such as population density, rateable value and the degree of need for certain kinds of local government services. In the last twenty years geographers have become interested in working out indices of rurality (Pacione 1984, ch. 1), especially in contexts such as planning. In this field there has been a noticeable shift from a 'polar' approach, which attempts to identify extremes of urban and rural, to one that is described as 'inductive' (Department of the Environment 1971; Cloke 1977; Cloke and Edwards 1986), which bases itself upon the measurement of selected variables to determine whether an area *inclines* towards the urban or rural pole. Under the latter approach, the measurement of such variables enables an index to be calculated which would show degrees of rurality. It would seem that the choice of variables tends to reflect the researchers' particular field of interest. So for planning purposes, criteria associated with patterns of employment may be selected, e.g. the percentage of males employed in rural industries; the percentage of resident population working in other areas (commuter population) (Department of Environment 1971). Other variables could also be sensibly taken into account (e.g. age structure of the population, migration, as indicators of population change and movement (Cloke 1977), certainly relevant for planning purposes and conceivably also in the context of criminal justice research). On the other hand, some sociologists have preferred to move on from the idea of a continuum between urban and rural to talk in terms of a series of *meshes*, recognizing common social variables in the extremes of urban and rural and suggesting a non-spatial analysis of geographical areas: 'the crux for sociologists is that the defining parameters of social problems are the same for rural as for urban areas' (Bailey 1975, 117).

The influence of both the 'inductive' and the 'meshing' or non-spatial approaches to area classification can be detected in the typologies which have been employed occasionally in recent years in the context of criminal justice research. For instance, the research by Tuck (1989) into 'non-metropolitan' violence based itself upon detailed typologies of different kinds of urban, suburban and rural areas which had been developed by market research analysts. These typologies, which divide areas of England, Wales and Scotland into 'families', further subdivided into 'clusters', are based largely on analysis of socio-economic conditions and can be seen as most relevant to research into the incidence and patterns of criminal behaviour. The typology avoids a broad division into urban and rural, and attempts a more revealing classification: for instance, 'mixed town and country with some industry', 'resort and retirement areas', 'areas with much local authority housing'. It is worth noting, for purposes of the present discussion, the main typology of a rural area which is put forward in this scheme[11] (the original source is Craig (1981)).

The typology identifies Family 2A as consisting of 'more rural areas'. The distinctive features of this family include a high proportion of the working population employed in agriculture, a mixed social structure, distinctive household tenure structure, an age structure tending towards the older rather than the younger, a high proportion of address changes and a small immigrant ('New Commonwealth') population. The four clusters of Family 2A break down its socio-economic character further still. Thus cluster 9: districts with a well-known medium-sized town which serves as a centre for a surrounding rural hinterland or even further afield; cluster 8: towns are smaller and less well known, so that the district is more dependent on agriculture and related activities. What can be noted about such description is that the label follows from the analysis of the socio-economic character of the area. It is not an exercise in looking to see what can be fitted into the category of

[11] For a summary, see Tuck (1989), Appendix A.

rural, but rather a process of looking at the character of the area in question and then deciding how to categorize it (and labels are mostly avoided, as can be seen from the practice of numbering 'families' and 'clusters'). There may be a lesson here, that the broad concept of the 'rural' may often be too elusive to be usable and that perhaps researchers should be seeking other, more accurate and meaningful terms for purposes of area classification.

Another system of area classification which has been used in criminal justice research in recent years is ACORN ('A Classification of Residential Neighbourhoods'), produced by CACI, a market and policy analysis consultancy.[12] ACORN employs cluster analysis to variables from the 1981 Census and has been increasingly employed in social research, for instance the 1983 and 1988 *British Crime Surveys* (Hough and Mayhew 1985; Mayhew, Elliot and Dowds 1989). The system is based on eleven neighbourhood groups which share characteristics of class, income and lifestyle – once again, in other words, socio-economic conditions which are relevant to research into the incidence and nature of criminal activity. For purposes of the *British Crime Surveys*, the ACORN classifications enabled the researchers to identify the immediate social environment of particular households and what kind of target for crime different areas offer. Respondents in the surveys were allocated to the most relevant ACORN area type and these data were then used to analyse rates of victimization. However, it should be noted for purposes of the present discussion that the ACORN classifications do not reflect very much the division between rural and urban. Only type 'A' ('agricultural areas: agricultural villages, area of farms and smallholdings') has any real rural flavour (and accounted for only 3.5 per cent of the 1988 *British Crime Survey* core sample). Other rural areas would have to be accommodated in some of the other types, which appear predominantly urban. For instance, type 'C' ('older housing of intermediate status') includes 'villages with non-farm employment'. Type 'J' ('affluent suburban housing') includes 'villages with wealthy older commuters' (but would these be regarded as rural villages?). Type 'K' ('better-off retirement areas') could conceivably include housing with rural characteristics, as an increasing number of relatively affluent and mobile people retire to country areas. This examination of the ACORN classification demonstrates again that a simple division between the urban and the rural may not be particularly relevant for much criminal justice research, which needs to focus on more

[12] For a further description of the ACORN classification, see Appendix G in the *1988 British Crime Survey* (Mayhew, Elliot and Dowds 1989).

specific area characteristics, some of which may be found in both urban and rural environments.

As a postscript to this discussion of area classification, something may be noted about the samples chosen by the authors of some of the following studies. For the most part, there will be little quarrel with the generally 'rural' character of the areas which have been investigated. Much of the material used by Lloyd, Hirst and Hurley is derived from mid- and west Wales, rural areas surely on most people's count. Robertshaw's study of Crown Courts ranges over a wider area, encompassing south-west England as well as many parts of Wales and he does admit to some doubts as to area classification. Indeed, Taunton in Somerset may appear less rural than Caernarfon in Gwynedd, but this would be to submit to a superficial impression. Although on the fringe of sparsely populated Snowdonia, Caernarfon Crown Court would also serve a relatively densely populated coastal hinterland, including the university town of Bangor, and the whole area would have a significant visiting population in the summer half of the year. Reverting now to the area classification of 'families' and 'clusters' referred to above, Caernarfon may belong as much to Family 2B ('resort and retirement areas') as to Family 2A ('more rural areas'). Equally, towns in the south-west of England such as Taunton and Yeovil would be located in cluster 11 ('more rural areas with industry') in Family 3 ('mixed town and country areas with some industry'). Much depends therefore upon the subject-matter of the inquiry. There may be a large geographical difference between the catchment area of a Crown Court and a magistrates' court and the former may be much more difficult to classify than the latter. It becomes increasingly clear therefore that the terms 'rural' and 'urban' have limited value in this context and that classifications which are more specifically appropriate to particular studies would be more beneficially used.

Rural Crime

Apart from the question of the relative incidence of crime in urban and rural areas, there is the separate issue of whether there are any distinctive kinds of rural crime. There are clearly some forms of criminal activity which to a large extent do occur in a 'rural' environment, such as poaching and animal 'rustling' and baiting, although this is not necessarily a question of distinct legal description. Many such offences are in a substantive legal sense familiar property offences which have been committed in a rural context. Strictly speaking, most poaching is not theft (since it is not possible to steal a wild creature not in captivity or reduced to another's possession).[13] None the less, there are a number of statutory offences analogous to theft, designed to protect other interests in wild life, enacted under such measures as the Poaching and Gaming Acts, the Protection of Birds Act 1954, the Deer Act 1963, the Conservation of Wild Creatures and Wild Plants Act 1975, and the Salmon and Freshwater Fisheries Act 1975. It may be true enough that these measures set out to deal with crime which is rural in its location, but it is not necessarily rural as regards its organization and perpetration.[14] Deer-slaying for example is usually 'big-time', 'professional' and not 'local' crime, so that once again the 'rural' epithet is brought into doubt.

The same point may be made about another area of criminality which has a rural dimension and has attracted a good deal of attention recently: fraud in relation to agricultural subsidies and other payments.[15] Clearly, there is some kind of rural background to this kind of offence, since the greater part of agriculture occurs in rural areas. But this is a situation in which the commonly used label tends to mislead (even more so when the more colloquial term 'farm fraud' is used). For, although the subject-matter of such transactions comprises agricultural produce, they are actually perpetrated on paper, in offices, at customs checkpoints, often by persons or business organizations based in large towns.[16] Such practices are much more accurately categorized as 'business crime' (which is suggestive of the urban rather than the rural) or, in many cases, 'international business crime' (suggestive of the cosmopolitan rather than the parochial). This example also serves to demonstrate that it is not easy in practice to disentangle rural and urban elements in some complex, highly organized forms of offending, especially in relation to property. Although undoubtedly some poaching is carried out by the local working class in rural areas, and some fraudulent claims are made by small farmers, the more serious and large-scale incidents of such offending are likely to be traced to professional criminals and businessmen who are by no means of a rustic character.

Even if it is difficult to find a convincing basis for the idea of a distinctive form of rural criminality, there are none the less worthwhile questions which can be posed about the phenomenon

[13] Theft Act 1968, s. 4(3).

[14] See e.g. Patrick Bishop, 'Massacre by moonlight', *The Observer*, 20 July 1980.

[15] House of Lords Committee on the European Communities, *Fraud Against the Community* (London, 1989); Ann Sherlock and Christopher Harding, 'Controlling fraud within the European Community', 1991 *European Law Review*, 20.

[16] Evidence given to the House of Lords Select Committee, n. 15 above.

of crime in the country, such as those already noted above in relation to incidence, 'dark figures' and the perception of offending. One quite obvious point that can be made about some rurally located crime concerns its environmental impact. 'Wildlife' offences can seriously undermine programmes of conservation and management of the environment. What is at issue in such cases therefore is a distinctive type of *interest* which the criminal law is being used to protect.[17] It is less clear that something like domestic violence is qualitatively or quantitatively different in rural and urban locations. The significance of the rural context would therefore seem to require a great deal more investigation and much may depend in this respect upon specific areas of criminal activity.

Rather than talk, then, of 'rural' crime, it is perhaps more meaningful to consider the occurrence and control of crime in the rural environment: the opportunity, or lack of opportunity, for more general forms of criminality, a particular colouring which may be given to the rural version of a certain offence and whether there is a different level of 'hidden' criminality in a rural context. The appropriate analogy here may be with the idea of 'international crime': there is little in the way of conduct which is distinctively international criminality, apart from the offence of piracy which, by definition, occurs beyond national boundaries. Yet there are many familiar types of offending which have an international dimension, and it is this which can turn them into something like a distinct offence, giving rise to different problems of enforcement. Poaching, rustling and smuggling may all be seen as areas of offending which, while not totally rural in character, often have a rural *dimension* which cannot be discounted in any discussion of the subject.

The Operation of Criminal Justice

So far more attention has been paid by researchers to the operation of the criminal justice system in rural contexts than to the nature of rural criminality (if there is such a distinct phenomenon). Indeed, it is as regards matters of procedure and enforcement that the more obvious differences between urban and rural may be identified. A major underlying problem arises from a combination of three factors inherent in the provision of criminal justice in more rural areas, two of which are geographical and the other administrative. In the first place, relatively low levels of population will justify relatively low funding and resources; but these have to be managed over large

[17] See e.g. William Howarth, 'Handling stolen goods and handling salmon', (1987) *Criminal Law Review* 460, for a discussion of the need for more specialized offences.

geographical areas. Put shortly, low resources are exacerbated by a sparse pattern of population, with its consequent enforcement demands. This situation is classically illustrated by the study by Hirst into implementation of the Police and Criminal Evidence Act 1984 (PACE) requirements for police custody in rural areas, where increased procedural demands could not be met by a commensurate increase in staffing levels.[18] The problem identified in that study is essentially organizational, but relates to rural and not urban policing areas. This problem of the stretching of limited resources was revealed in another context by the study made by Jones (1990) into the use of probation with a condition for psychiatric treatment in north Wales. There the limited resources in terms of psychiatric treatment resulted in a situation in which the great majority of such orders relied on the services of a very small number of doctors based in just one hospital, a factor which appeared to inhibit the making of that kind of order in the first place.[19] The solution to this kind of problem is straightforward in theory (increased resources) but far from so in practice. Need for funding in the criminal justice system is largely based on case-load, rather than the logistical difficulties in dealing with that case-load. However, it is difficult to see how, for instance, the problem of dealing with arrested offenders under PACE in sparsely populated areas can be effectively addressed without some increase in the level of resources.

The issues identified in Lloyd's study of magistrates courts are of a different nature, and relate not so much to resource provision in the narrow sense as to the quality of the system of justice which can be provided by such courts. The disadvantages associated with rural benches include the greater likelihood of a narrow social composition and slow turnover in membership and a limited case-load in terms of both the range of offences and number of cases, resulting in a limited experience in matters of both trial and sentence.[20] (Interestingly, in this connection, Robertshaw has used low case-load as a *criterion* for his selection of rural Crown Courts.)[21] The danger then is that such courts may display a narrow viewpoint, be less susceptible to new developments in law and policy and be unduly cautious or conservative in choice of sentence. If such possible tendencies in magistrates' decision-making are combined with some of the resource problems mentioned above,

[18] See below, p. 92.

[19] Gail Jones (1990), 79–80, but note the plan mentioned there to set up a greater number of smaller treatment centres in different parts of Clwyd and Gwynedd.

[20] See below, p. 65.

[21] See below, p. 52.

the hypothesis may be advanced, for example, that the chance of a rural defendant being dealt with by a psychiatric probation order is very much less than an urban counterpart, even assuming that the measure would be equally appropriate in both cases. It is in such respects that there appears to be some significant distinction between urban and rural criminal justice which is also cause for some concern.

Inevitably, the most likely response to the problem of small rural benches is a policy of reorganization into a smaller number of larger courts, a process to some extent already under way. Yet this may in turn lead to some of the practical difficulties of distance which have become evident in relation to police custody. Moreover, reducing the number of magistrates' courts would be also to reduce the level of local accountability, which is seen as an important element in magistrates' justice. However, it should be noted that distance between courts need not in itself be a problem, if communications are effective in a rural area; fast roads and a good provision of public transport would go some way to offset the loss of a more local court. It is in relation to this kind of situation that pure geographical factors such as distance and population may not provide a complete picture, and that some reference should therefore be made to such matters as communications and the level of public services. The research by Henshaw (1988) into the effectiveness of magistrates' justice demonstrated that county areas which were at first sight comparable in general geographical terms none the less differed as regards the effectiveness of magistrates' court provision,[22] and that organizational, as distinct from geographical, factors could be decisive. While in some situations the level of resources may be an inescapable issue, it would be misleading to assert that generally the solution to such practical problems is necessarily a matter of the amount of funding for the criminal justice system.

Robertshaw's comparison of Crown Court outcomes in rural and urban areas reflects less on organizational problems (apart from his consideration of the level of delay) than on any differences in decision-making at successive stages of the process (for instance, as to plea, acquittal and sentence). The fact that his study does not in most respects confidently point to general differences between rural and urban proceedings perhaps reinforces the conclusion that the real distinctions are organizational and administrative rather than in substantive policy. There is, however, one intriguing finding in his research: rural defendants appeared more likely to plead not guilty (had an 'appetite for trial'), and a relatively high number of these rural not-guilty pleaders were acquitted. This would be worth

[22] Henshaw (1988).

testing further over a larger sample and longer period, and does suggest some possible differences in defence strategy as between proceedings in rural and urban courts. Any such differences are less likely to relate to the nature of the offences being tried or the perception of the Crown Court judges (neither of which are likely to have a distinctively rural element) than to factors such as the nature of legal advice or the perception of juries' decision-making, both of which could conceivably be affected by local circumstances. The relevant question to pose may therefore be: are 'rural' defence lawyers more optimistic because 'rural' juries are seen to be more favourably disposed towards defendants?

The study by Hurley examines a very different aspect of criminal justice, non-statutory provision for offenders and for victims of crime, and the focus on such provision in the mid-Wales area suggests some specific problems faced by agencies located in more rural areas. The decline in the ability of NACRO (National Association for the Care and Resettlement of Offenders) to maintain its programme in most parts of Wales may to some extent be linked to the vulnerability of small-scale operations at a time of retraction and the familiar problem of resources having to be extended over a wide geographical area. The implication of this study is that rural areas, being among the first to suffer when resources become scarce, are in effect viewed at a low level of priority in policy-making which is worked out nationally and perhaps primarily in accordance with urban models. In contrast, victim support schemes have been relatively flourishing during the same period. A significant factor in this respect may be the degree of autonomy enjoyed by local victim support schemes: whereas for NACRO programmes 'a decision taken further up the hierarchy is final; for a Victim Support scheme its volunteer composition may be its power base',[23] and victim support has a much greater tradition of local fund-raising. Difficulties may be substantive as well as organizational, however. In particular, Hurley raises the issue of confidentiality as a problem in the rural context. In relation to NACRO's efforts, finding training places for offenders could be more difficult compared to the more anonymous urban environment, since there was a greater chance that a rural community would be aware of both the identity of offenders and the nature of their offences. Confidentiality in fact is likely to be a more widespread problem: the same would be true, for instance, of work placements under community service orders in rural areas.

Taken as a whole, however, the chapters which follow here suggest that organizational and administrative problems are the

[23] See below, p. 116.

most significant in the context of rural criminal justice. There are a number of issues concerning resources and difficulties in management which derive from rural social and geographical factors, and a perhaps inevitable tendency in governmental policy to give lower priority to rural areas. Some of these issues are not simply resource problems within the criminal justice system: they interrelate with other areas of policy, such as health and transport, in which central government provision is likely to be directed towards more populous areas. At the same time, although under-funding is a pervasive theme, there are also separate predicaments. Low case-loads (a basic element in low funding) result in limited experience for those operating the system, and this may then have consequences for the content of decision-making in terms of a less responsive and sophisticated process at a number of levels. There is no obvious way out of this dilemma, which seems to confirm what is already seen by many as a fact of rural life – that it lags behind the towns in most areas of economic and social development. Policies which attempt to change this in effect serve to make what is rural less so. This is not to say that studies which identify problems of resources, case-load and distance are trite. They remain problems, which need to be addressed. But it may not add very much in practice to stress that they are problems of the rural environment. Few readers will probably be surprised to learn that.

The Way Forward for Criminal Justice Research into Rural Areas

The purpose of this discussion has been to report on the level of research in the criminal justice field in the rural environment and on the problems of defining the parameters of such research and exploring its utility. Many of the conclusions are unsurprising: that existing research has focused predominantly on indisputably urban areas; that there may be distinctive problems as regards the operation of criminal justice agencies in rural areas; that there is little evidence (mainly because there has been little study made of this question) of a distinctively rural criminality. Most significantly, perhaps, the whole issue of distinguishing between urban and rural can be shown to be problematical, and it may be that for many purposes of social research that terminology is not very helpful. Many parts of the UK are, according to the criteria most frequently employed, a mixture of the rural and the urban. Area classifications which have been developed for social science and policy research are very much related to more specific geographical and socio-economic characteristics. It may be argued that *a priori* labelling should be avoided and that, as researchers move beyond the clearly urban ('metropolitan'?) environment, specific research concerns and objectives should dictate the kind of area descriptions which are used. If a general label is necessary, it may be that 'non-urban' or 'non-metropolitan' would be more appropriate descriptions than 'rural'.

On the other hand, conceptual and definitional hurdles should not dissuade researchers from the utility of future (or perhaps, more accurately, new) inquiries into crime and criminal justice outside the cities and the suburbs. For it is difficult to discard the impression that national policy in the UK on crime and the criminal justice system is based upon a concern with inner city and suburban crime. Agencies working outside these areas confront resource and organizational difficulties which may not be very surprising but are none the less real, and the existence of these problems does at least beg some questions about the use of conventional criteria for the distribution of resources and the genesis of policy from a national centre.

As far as the idea of 'rural crime' is concerned, it remains the case that little specific knowledge has been collected. It would seem difficult to maintain that there are clearly differentiated urban and rural offences or types of offender, especially with the incursion of some organized crime into the rural environment. Yet a number of worthwhile questions may be asked about crime in more rural areas and the response to such offending. It could be asked, for instance, whether an issue such as domestic violence constitutes a different phenomenon in rural areas: is there a different rural subculture which would affect attitudes towards such violence, in turn conditioning responses within civil society and the level of reporting to, and involvement on the part of, state agencies? Is it easier for such offending to go undetected in rural areas? Do magistrates and juries in such areas react differently to offences of violence, so affecting legal strategies in relation to prosecution, choice of plea or argument in relation to sentence? It would at least be worth following up some of these questions since it is possible that such inquiry may reveal some differences in attitude and perception which may then inform our overall understanding of the nature and working of the criminal justice system.

Bibliography

Bailey, J. (1975) *Social Theory for Planning* (London, 1975).

Baldwin, J. R. and McConville, M. (1977) *Negotiated Justice* (London, 1977).

Baldwin, J. R. (1985) *Pre-trial Justice* (London 1985).

Blacksell, M., Economides, K. and Watkins, C. (eds.) (1991) *Justice Outside the City: Access to Legal Services in Rural Britain* (London, 1991).

Cloke, P. J. (1977) 'An index of rurality for England and Wales', *Regional Studies*, 11 (1977).

Cloke, P. J. and Edwards, G. (1986) 'Rurality in England and Wales 1981: a replication of the 1971 index', *Regional Studies*, 20 (1986), 289.

Craig, J. (1981) *A 1981 Socio-economic Classification of Local Health Authority Areas in Great Britain* (London, 1981).

Department of the Environment (1971) *The Nature of Rural Areas of England and Wales* (internal working paper) (London, 1971).

Doherty, M. J. and East, R. (1985) 'Bail decisions in magistrates' courts', 25, *B. J. Crim*, 251 (1985).

Henshaw, Lesley (1988) *The Governance and Organisation of the Magistrates Courts Service*, unpublished PhD thesis, University of Wales (1988).

Hough, Mike and Mayhew, Pat (1985) *Taking Account of Crime*, Home Office Research Study no. 85 (London, 1985).

Jones, Gail (1990) 'The use and effectiveness of the probation order with a condition for psychiatric treatment in north Wales', 20, *Cambrian Law Review*, 63 (1990).

Mayhew, Pat, Elliot, David and Dowds, Lizanne (1989) *The 1988 British Crime Survey*, Home Office Research Study no. 111 (London, 1989).

Pacione, M. (1984) *Rural Geography* (London, 1984).

Tuck, Mary (1989) *Drinking and Disorder: A Study of Non-metropolitan Violence*, Home Office Research Study no. 108 (London, 1989).

Vennard, Julie (1982) *Contested Trials in Magistrates' Courts*, Home Office Research Study no. 71 (London, 1982).

Walsh, Dermot (1980) *Break-ins: Burglary from Private Houses* (London, 1980).

Zander, Michael (1979) 'The operation of the Bail Act in London magistrates' courts', 1979 *New Law Journal*, 108.

4

Rural Crown Courts: are they different?

PAUL ROBERTSHAW

Introduction

This chapter examines a series of outcomes in the 'rural' courts in the Crown Court, the superior part of the criminal justice system of England and Wales, where trial by jury is obligatory for all contested cases. The methods used are largely statistical and comparative, so it must be said at the outset that certain important qualitative aspects of justice, including 'atmosphere' such as 'homilies' – sermons, denunciations and moralizing by sentencing judges – are missing from this study. Another admission, or rather question, is whether the focus is on the correct courts. No doubt other contributors and the editor of this volume will have helpful things to say on this score. For my part, I must admit that if my characterization of the 'rural' is inaccurate, then I will have included the urban with the rural and possibly made the error of comparing like with like if too many 'rural' courts have been left in my comparative group; so I have played rather safe.

To come to the point, the 'population' from which my selection has been made is the sixty-four courts in the Wales-and-Chester, Western, Northern, North-Eastern and Midlands-and-Oxford Circuits (with the addition of Aylesbury, Cambridge and Reading to complete their Crown Prosecution Service areas). Those selected are entirely from the Wales-and-Chester and Western Circuits: Barnstaple, Bodmin-Truro, Caernarfon, Carmarthen, Dorchester, Haverfordwest, Newport (Isle of Wight), Salisbury, Taunton and Welshpool. My primary criteria were openly subjective – including ignorance, for example, of Grimsby and Lincoln. These criteria included some notion of population intensity, isolation from other centres, and agricultural predominance. Even this latter category is slippery: Welshpool's market is today a car park. Merthyr Tydfil is effectively de-industrialized and adjacent to the Brecon Beacons National Park – yet I have omitted it. There is also the problem of grouped court centres exemplified by Bodmin–Truro; Carlisle may be an urban centre but it includes a number of undoubtedly rural centres such as Kirkby Lonsdale and Sedbergh whose statistics could not be extracted; I had particular difficulty with Worcester–Hereford.

An objective criterion was important at the margin: case-load volume per annum. This presents rather than eases problems of method. To start with, two prime candidates could not be studied because their statistics were minuscule: Dolgellau and Devizes. Secondly, I had to make a choice whether to keep the volume up by including the minority of more serious remanded cases (ranging from 12.2 per cent at Newport (Isle of Wight) to 36.4 per cent at Caernarfon, both in 1987) or to concentrate on the typical bailed cases. I chose the latter course because it is more rigorous and because none of the courts chosen ever had a viable minimum sample (fixed by experience of statistical significance testing at twenty-five) of not-guilty pleas by remanded defendants, and only Caernarfon with Bodmin–Truro and Taunton had viable samples of guilty pleas by remanded defendants. There *is* a risk in this, because the proportion of remanded 'serious' cases could be argued to contribute to the atmosphere, self-perception and tariff levels of a court, especially those with small case-loads: more than a quarter of cases were remanded in custody pre-trial at Taunton, Salisbury and Caernarfon in 1987. In the second year, selected for study of patterns and continuity, 1989, the same occurred at Barnstaple, Caernarfon, Haverfordwest and Salisbury. Nevertheless this is a choice I would defend. Since I was unable to separate out types of offence from my data, remand was the only indicator of the level of 'seriousness' available. To lump such cases, however important, with the routine fare of a court, when I could not mount any serious comparison of the remand cases with those of the courts, would have been a mistake leading to distortion. One surprising benefit survived these difficulties of selection: the ten courts are not exclusively from Tier III, the lowest level, of the Crown Court structure: Caernarfon and Bodmin-Truro are Tier I, Dorchester and Welshpool are Tier II, and Taunton is a Tier III town.

I now present tables 4.1 and 4.2, which simply display the volume of not-guilty and guilty pleas for bailed and remanded defendants for these courts. They also introduce the reader to a further method

Table 4.1 1987 Volume: *bailed* (63 courts), *remanded* (%)
(NGP + GP: total)

QI	[*Dolgellau*	2 + 12 : 14]		
	Welshpool	(14) + 25 : 39	(0 + 10 : 10)	(20.4)
	Salisbury	(19) + 39 : 58	(2 + 20 : 22)	(27.5)
	Haverfordwest	26 + 35 : 61	(0 + 13 : 13)	(17.6)
	Dorchester	46 + 35 : 81	(10 + 13 : 23)	(22.1)
	Newport (IoW)	50 + 51 : 101	(4 + 10 : 14)	(12.2)
	Barnstaple	41 + 86 : 127	(3) + 28 : 31	(19.6)
	Caernarfon	47 + 112 : 159	(10) + 87 : 91	(36.4)
	Carmarthen	82 + 90 : 172	(8) + 28 : 36	(17.3)
	Knutsford	80 + 192 : 272		
	Swindon	118 + 187 : 305		
	Warrington	84 + 250 : 334		
	Taunton	80 + 264 : 344	(9) + 107 : 116	(25.2)
	Carlisle	121 + 229 : 350		
	Bournemouth	154 + 212 : 366		
	Cambridge	91 + 286 : 377		
QII	*Merthyr Tydfil*	175 + 220 : 395		
	Grimsby	98 + 304 : 402		
	Shrewsbury	104 + 320 : 424		
	Bodmin-Truro	134 + 292 : 426	(13) + 90 : 103	(19.5)
M	*Winchester*	269 + 403 : 672	*Southampton*	43 + 215 : 258
QIV	*Leeds*	775 + 3340 : 4115	*Manchester*	226 + 1532 : 1758

Table 4.2 1989 Volume: *bailed* (63 courts), *remanded* (%)
(NGP + GP: total)

QI	Haverfordwest	(13) + 30 : 43	(3 + 14 : 17)	(28.3)
	Welshpool	(20) + (24) : 44	(1 + 7 : 8)	(15.4)
	Salisbury	(21) + 26 : 47	(1 + 18 : 19)	(28.8)
	Barnstaple	25 + 48 : 73	(2) + 36 : 38	(34.2)
	Dorchester	64 + 64 : 128	(10) + (22) : 32	(20.0)
	Carmarthen	49 + 83 : 132	(5) + 27 : 32	(19.5)
	Newport (IoW)	75 + 111 : 186	(4) + 31 : 35	(15.1)
	Caernarfon	71 + 139 : 210	(18) + 92 : 110	(34.4)
	Taunton	102 + 282 : 384	(1) + 79 : 80	(17.2)
QII	Bodmin-Truro	115 + 314 : 429	(11) + 100 : 111	(20.6)
M	*Coventry*	110 + 421 : 531	*Oxford*	(23) + 96: 119
QIV	*Liverpool*	117 + 2768 : 2885	*Manchester*	194 + 1399: 1593

used, their division into quartiles of those courts having more than twenty-five cases available for comparison, especially between the low and high quartiles. (Occasionally where the numbers dip below twenty-five for a particular selected court and where the percentages are not freakish I display them in brackets). To save space I shall display courts outside the selected ten only where they are at the pole or median of a table, but I shall always indicate the number of courts that would appear in the table if printed in full; but, the reader is reminded, only the majority of typical bailed cases are considered here; the focus is on the routine rather than the outrageous.

The Defendants

Because of the form of the data relied on (annualized returns to the Lord Chancellor's Department)[1] there is, regrettably, no breakdown possible for type of crime – even the bail/remand distinction is subject to the vagaries of local discretion – so all one can say at the outset is that all the defendants in the cases studied and courts compared were free on bail pre-trial.

In addition we can consider something else about defendants' condition pre-trial, namely how long they have to wait. The data give the level of weeks between committal and commencement of trial. It is not fully standardized since we do not know how long elapsed between charge and committal, but at least these are reliable minimum figures. From these I have selected a delay criterion of percentage of cases waiting for more than twenty weeks

Table 4.3 *Waiting time*: excess 20 weeks % *guilty pleas* (bailed, 62 courts)

1987			1989		
QI	0	Carmarthen	QI	0	Carmarthen
	0	Salisbury		3.3	Haverfordwest
	0	Haverfordwest			
QII	5.4	Caernarfon	QII	7.3	Bodmin-Truro
				(8.3)	Welshpool
M	5.7	*Winchester*	M	9.2	*Aylesbury*
QIII	7.9	Bodmin-Truro	QIII	10.4	Barnstaple
				11.1	Salisbury
QIV	14.3	Dorchester	QIV	15.1	Caernarfon
	17.4	Taunton		18.0	Newport IoW
	33.7	Barnstaple		18.8	Taunton
	44.0	Welshpool			
	54.9	Newport (IoW)		29.7	Dorchester
Range	54.9			29.7	
Rural	54.9			29.7	

[1] I am grateful to the LCD for permission to use these returns; all calculations from and interpretations of them are my responsibility.

(five months). One's expectation might be that courts with low-volume case-loads would have low rates of delay. Tables 4.3 and 4.4 for bailed guilty and not-guilty pleas show that these rural courts cover the entire range for both pleas for both years. How particular courts fit into the picture is another issue which we will return to later. We can also dispense with the hypothesis that rural Welsh courts are generally different from their English counterparts. The other known characteristics of these defendants is their plea and willingness to stand trial for maintaining a not-guilty plea. We can also relate this to the delay factor.

It can be seen from table 4.5 that a generalization can be made for both years. Rural defendants plead not guilty more than their urban bailed counterparts. Since five Crown Prosecution Service areas are involved, it is difficult to ascribe this feature to prosecution practice or policy, and I have no qualitative information on defendants' relations with local solicitors. The only other relevant information available is that already presented on delay: Taunton defendants have a lower, Quartile II rate in both years, and Salisbury, Welshpool, Carmarthen, Newport (Isle of Wight) and Dorchester consistently high rates in Quartile IV in both years.

We can see from table 4.4 that Carmarthen consistently avoided delay (O, Q1) and that Caernarfon and Taunton were plagued by it (QIV). There are not sufficient data from which to draw conclusions, so one can simply note that in two courts there were strong correlations between speed and trial (not-guilty plea) and vice

Table 4.4 *Waiting time*: *excess 20 weeks % not-guilty pleas* (bailed, 61 courts)

1987			1989		
QI	0	Carmarthen	QI	0	Carmarthen
	0	Haverfordwest			
QII	13.0	Dorchester		16.0	Barnstaple
	(15.8)	Salisbury			
M	20.0	*Exeter*	M	20.6	Bodmin-Truro
			QIII	25.0	Dorchester
				(30.0)	Welshpool
QIV	34.0	Caernarfon	QIV	36.3	Taunton
	34.3	Bodmin-Truro		(42.9)	Salisbury
	52.5	Taunton			
	61.0	Barnstaple			
	62.0	Newport (IoW)		54.9	Caernarfon
Range	62.0			54.9	
Rural	62.0			54.9	

Table 4.5 *Not-guilty plea rates* (bailed defendants, 62 courts) %

1987			Tier	1989			Tier
QI	11.1	*Durham*	III	QI	9.7	*Doncaster*	III
QII	23.3	Taunton	III	QII	26.6	Taunton	III
					26.8	Bodmin-Truro	I
M	25.3	*Bolton*	III	M	27.5	*Cambridge*	III
QIII	29.6	Caernarfon	I	QIII	30.2	Haverfordwest	III
	31.5	Bodmin-Truro	I				
	32.3	Barnstaple	III				
QIV	32.8	Salisbury	III	QIV	33.9	Caernarfon	I
	35.9	Welshpool	II		34.2	Barnstaple	III
	42.6	Haverfordwest	III		37.9	Carmarthen	II
	47.7	Carmarthen	II		40.3	Newport (IoW)	III
	49.5	Newport (IoW)	III		44.7	Salisbury	III
					45.5	Welshpool	II
	56.8	Dorchester	II		50.0	Dorchester	II
Range	45.7				40.3		
Rural	33.5				23.4		

versa, which was not contradicted by clear evidence regarding the other courts. This fits one's expectations regarding administrative imperatives and court practice. Even if it is a numerically weak fit, the fact remains that, for whatever reason, rural defendants do seem to be different in their appetite for trial. We shall see later whether this faith in judges and rural juries is justified.

Judges in Rural Crown Courts

At Trial

It is frequently forgotten that juries do not get to their deliberations and verdicts on every not-guilty plea that enters the courts. A certain amount are filtered out, often at the prosecution's initiative, by judicial discharge before a jury has even been empanelled. Here the judge will have been convinced that the trial would fail through defects, particularly in evidence. In addition during trial, and more dramatically, the judge may intervene to direct the jury to acquit, typically when key witnesses fail or are demolished, or when the facts disclose no breach of the law charged.

We cannot characterize the judges at these courts as 'rural' in the way that we would describe magistrates rooted in a particular community – even Recorders are unlikely to have such immediate connections with the court they are assigned to. So at most we can

Table 4.6 *Judicially discharged at trial* (bailed defendants, 61 courts)

1987			1989		
QI	6.3	*Knutsford*	QI	1.1	*Teesside*
				5.6	Caernarfon
				(9.5)	Salisbury
				14.1	Dorchester
QII	13.0	Dorchester	QII	20.0	Barnstaple
	14.0	Newport (IoW)		(20.0)	Welshpool
M	15.9	*Stoke*	M	20.2	*Bolton*
QIII	17.0	Caernarfon	QIII	26.1	Bodmin-Truro
	19.5	Carmarthen			
QIV	22.4	Bodmin-Truro	QIV	28.0	Newport (IoW)
	24.4	Barnstaple			
	25.0	Taunton			
	26.9	Haverfordwest			
	(31.6)	Salisbury		34.7	Carmarthen
	38.0	*Doncaster*		37.3	Taunton
Range	31.7			36.2	
Rural	18.6			31.7	

characterize them in other relevant ways, in this instance by their degree of interventionism, and again we can relate that to the level of not-guilty pleas and delay.

We can see from table 4.6 that there is a tendency for higher levels of pre-empanellment discharge at rural Crown Courts. This is more marked in 1987 than 1989. Two courts are consistent: Dorchester (QII) and Taunton (QIV); in addition Bodmin–Truro and Carmarthen are consistently above the median (QIII, QIV).

From table 4.7 we can see that the general tendency is for directed acquittals to lie in the opposite direction, that is below the median, with Carmarthen and Newport (Isle of Wight) in Quartile I. Bodmin–Truro is the exception, being consistently above the median (QIII, QIV). This is suggestive that, despite the apparent tendency, there may be no necessary correlation between high discharge and low directed acquittal rates, and vice versa, because Carmarthen and Bodmin–Truro were both high discharge courts.

We can categorize courts as prima facie interventionist by combining their discharge and directed acquittal rates for each year and establishing consistency (see table 4.8). It can be seen that Barnstaple, Bodmin–Truro and Taunton are consistently interventionist courts. With Taunton this may involve a causal connection between the high rate of delay and high pre-empanellment discharge rate. This leaves Barnstaple and Bodmin–Truro as interventionist

Table 4.7 *Directed acquittals during trial* (bailed defendants, 60 courts)

1987			1989		
QI	0	*Doncaster*	QI	0	*Coventry*
	0	Newport (IoW)		(0)	Salisbury
	0	Carmarthen		1.8	Dorchester
				3.1	Carmarthen
	5.1	Caernarfon		5.6	Newport (IoW)
QII	(5.3)	Haverfordwest	QII	(10.0)	Barnstaple
	6.7	Taunton		10.4	Caernarfon
	7.5	Dorchester			
M	8.8	*Warrington*	M	11.2	*Chester*
QIII	9.7	Barnstaple	QIII	12.9	Bodmin-Truro
QIV	13.5	Bodmin-Truro	QIV	18.8	Taunton
	21.5	*Carlisle*		24.2	*Peterborough*
Range	21.5			24.2	
Rural	13.5			18.8	

Table 4.8 *Discharges and directed acquittals combined*

	1987		1989	
Barnstaple	24.4 + 9.7	: 34.1	20 + (10)	: 30.0
Bodmin-Truro	22.4 + 13.5	: 35.9	26.1 + 12.9	: 39.0
Taunton	25.0 + 6.7	: 31.7	37.3 + 18.8	: 56.1
Newport (IoW)	14.0 + 0	: 14.0	28.0 + 5.6	: 33.6
Carmarthen	19.5 + 0	: 19.5	34.7 + 3.1	: 37.8
(Dorchester		: 20.5		15.9)
(Caernarfon		: 22.1		16.0)
Salisbury, Haverfordwest, Welshpool: insufficient data				

in that no administrative factors account for their high rates.

Rural Juries

Table 4.9 provides an excellent depiction of the mystery of the jury, rural or urban, so zealously over-protected by section 8 of the Contempt of Court Act 1981.[2] In 1987 the range of acquittals

[2] The author was involved in lobbying for the repeal or amendment of that section. The Courts (Research) Bill was sponsored by Dr Mike Woodcock MP and promoted by the Bar Council. Clause 2 contained the reform. It was debated in the Commons on 21/2/1991 and passed, after favourable discussion, 22–0. However, the Bill, being a Private Member's Bill failed under the Quorum rules. But see now Recommendation 1 of the Royal Commission on Criminal Justice Cm 2263 (1993) ch. 1, para. 8.

Table 4.9 *Jury acquittals %* (bailed defendants, 60 courts)

1987			1989		
QI	5.6	*Portsmouth*	QI	(15.8)	Salisbury
	14.3	Taunton		25.5	Newport (IoW)
	21.4	Barnstaple			
	21.6	Dorchester			
QII	27.0	Caernarfon	QII	31.1	Bodmin-Truro
	28.8	Carmarthen		31.5	Dorchester
				(33.3)	Barnstaple
M	29.1	*Teesside*	M	35.1	*Grimsby*
QIII			QIII	36.5	Taunton
QIV	34.9	Newport (IoW)	QIV	45.0	Caernarfon
	36.7	Bodmin-Truro			
	(44.4)	Haverfordwest			
	48.4	*Warrington*		48.4	Carmarthen
Range	42.8			32.6	
Rural	30.1			32.6	

avoids the extremes (42.8 per cent) but still covers 30.1 per cent from Taunton to Haverfordwest. In 1989 the entire range is covered for all sixty Courts, from Salisbury to Caernarfon and Carmarthen. Moreover within each court there are considerable swings between years, especially Caernarfon (18.0 per cent) Carmarthen (19.6 per cent) and Taunton (22.2 per cent). There are no consistently high or low acquitting juries in these rural courts.

There is one further set of information, highly relevant to stereotypes of rustic justice: pastoral cohesion and consensus on the one hand, and stubborn individualism on the other. This is the rate of majority verdicts on conviction. (Since we do not have the sophistication of the Scots not-proven verdict in England or Wales, figures are not published on majority acquittals). Because of attrition of cases through the three varieties of acquittal, the data are a little thin in table 4.10, but enough to reinforce the representation of extreme diversity, with the entire range of 28.6 per cent accounted for by this rural sample in 1987 and a much narrower range of 8.1 per cent out of 26.4 per cent in 1989. Caernarfon appears to be a high consensus town, and Dorchester considerably lower. Possibly Caernarfon juries put their reasonable doubts into their high acquittal rate in 1989? But what can one make of Dorchester and Newport (Isle of Wight) juries in 1987?

The data also allow us to examine the relationship between judges and juries. Does a high judicial rate of intervention clear the decks for the jury to concentrate on the difficult cases, or does it, especially

Table 4.10 *Majority verdicts on conviction* % (bailed defendants, 58 courts)

1987			1989		
QI	(0)	Caernarfon	QI	0	*Bolton*
				3.0	Caernarfon
	6.7	Carmarthen		(4.5)	Newport (IoW)
QII	8.0	Taunton	QII	7.4	Taunton
	10.2	Bodmin-Truro		7.7	Bodmin-Truro
M	11.4	*Chester*	M	9.3	*Preston*
QIII			QIII	(11.1)	Dorchester
				26.4	*Winchester*
QIV	26.9	Dorchester			
	28.6	Newport (IoW)			
Range	28.6			26.4	
Rural	28.6			8.1	

the visible directed acquittals, have an exemplar effect? If we consider first the general rate of intervention (table 4.8) for each year separately: Barnstaple, Bodmin–Truro, Haverfordwest and Taunton in 1987, and Bodmin–Truro, Carmarthen, Newport (Isle of Wight) and Taunton in 1989, one can find no patterns whatsoever: jury acquittals being in Quartiles I for Barnstaple and Taunton and in Quartile IV for Bodmin–Truro and Haverfordwest in 1987, and in Quartiles I for Newport (Isle of Wight), II for Bodmin–Truro, III for Taunton and IV for Carmarthen in 1989. If we restrict ourselves to the visible directed acquittals (not necessarily visible to the same juries) in Quartile IV we can observe Bodmin–Truro in 1987 and Taunton in 1989. Here we have suggestive evidence that there is a correlation between above–median acquittals by juries and high rates of acquittals by judges directed to juries, that is: there may be an exemplar effect at work.

Sentencing

Only one measure of judicial practice will be used here, the trite but well tried one of the custodial (including partially suspended custody) rate. Separate tables have, however, been constructed for those defendants pleading guilty and for those convicted after trial of a not-guilty plea (tables 4.11 and 4.12).

For guilty pleas there is for both years a tendency, not strongly pronounced, for lower rates of custodial sentence in these rural courts; certainly there are far more courts in Quartile I than IV. Sentences are the typical outcome for all criminal courts – both magistrates and the Crown Court – and so constitute an important

Table 4.11 *Custodial (including partially suspended) sentences % bailed defendants pleading guilty* (62 courts)

1987			1989		
QI	31.1	Carmarthen	QI	10.8	*Preston*
	31.4	Dorchester		14.6	Barnstaple
	34.3	Haverfordwest		23.4	Newport (IoW)
	36.0	Welshpool		26.2	Taunton
	36.4	Taunton			
				31.3	Dorchester
				31.3	Carmarthen
QII	42.5	Bodmin-Truro	QII	35.0	Bodmin-Truro
	43.1	Newport (IoW)			
M	44.3	*Leicester*	M	39.0	*Derby*
QIII	48.7	Salisbury	QIII	40.0	Haverfordwest
QIV	51.8	Caernarfon	QIV		
	52.3	Barnstaple		59.0	Caernarfon
	60.1	*Coventry*		(70.8)	Welshpool
Range	29.0			60.0	
Rural	21.2			24.4	

Table 4.12 *Custodial (including partially suspended) sentences % bailed defendants convicted at trial on N-G plea* (59 courts)

1987			1989		
QI	29.8	Carmarthen	QI	15.2	Taunton
	(35.0)	Barnstaple		21.1	Newport (IoW)
	36.0	Newport (IoW)			
				35.0	Bodmin-Truro
QII	48.3	Dorchester	QII		
	50.0	Bodmin-Truro			
M	51.7	*Sheffield*	M	50.0	*Dorchester*
QIII			QIII		
QIV	64.7	Taunton	QIV	64.7	Caernarfon
	82.3	Caernarfon		76.2	*Mold*
Range	52.5			61.0	
Rural	52.5			49.5	

indicator of the quality of rural justice. A minority of courts are consistent in their practice wherever in the spectrum it may be: Carmarthen, Dorchester and Taunton in the lowest Quartile I, Bodmin–Truro (Tier I), around the median for the sixty-two courts and Caernarfon (also Tier I) in the highest Quartile IV.

The sample shrinks for those convicted at trial, but in both years covers a very wide range of 52.8 per cent from Carmarthen to Caernarfon in 1987 and 49.5 per cent from Taunton to Caernarfon in 1989. Caernarfon remains consistent as a court whose judges produce custodial outcomes; Dorchester is consistently close to the median for the fifty-nine courts examined.

One other feature must be mentioned here, but not followed up as it is the subject of much fuller study elsewhere,[3] except to say that it is definitely not a phenomenon restricted to rural courts or bailed defendants. Those courts in the lowest Quartile I for custodial sentences of defendants convicted at trial after a not-guilty pleas consistently impose such sentences at a *higher* rate for those pleading guilty, notably Barnstaple and Newport (Isle of Wight) in 1987 and Taunton in 1989.

Are Rural Crown Courts Different?

There is one simple answer to this question, but not perhaps to the way in which it was first intended: rural Crown courts are different from each other. That will have become apparent from every table presented, and can be reinforced by thumbnail sketches of 'adjacent' courts.

Carmarthen

No excessive delay at all (QI GP and NGP 1987 and 1989), despite high rates of not-guilty pleas (QIV 1987/9), but perhaps because of relatively low remand rates (17.5 per cent; 19.5 per cent). The rates of judicial discharge were not consistent, but directed acquittals were very low (QI, 1987/9). Jury acquittal rates were not consistent. For defendants pleading guilty, custodial sentences were low (QI 1987/9 and 1987 for NGP convicted).

Caernarfon

Consistent delay for not-guilty pleas (QIV 1987 and 1989, also for GP 1989), perhaps because of above-median rates of NGP pleas (QIII 1987, QIV 1989), but more probably because of the high remand rates (36.4 per cent 1987, 34.4 per cent 1989). Judicial intervention whether as discharge or directed acquittal was never high. Jury acquittals varied considerably between the years but were united by the very low rates of majority convictions (QI 1987/9). Custodial sentences were *de rigueur* whether for guilty pleas or convicted at trial of these bailed defendants (QIV 1987/9, QIV 1987/9).

[3] 31 Howard Journal of Criminal Justice (1992), 53–75.

Barnstaple

A tendency towards delay, not consistent (QIV 1987, QIII 1989 GP; QIV 1989 NGP), possibly related to above-median not-guilty plea rates (QIII 1987, QIV 1989); the remand rates were not consistent (19.6 per cent 1987; 34.2 per cent 1989). Although the rates of judicial intervention were not consistent, they were not low (QIV 1987, QII 1989; QIII 1987, QII 1989). Jury acquittals were below the median (QI 1987, QII 1989). For guilty pleas there were very large variations in the custodial rate between years (QIV 1987, QI 1989).

Taunton

A court marked by consistent delay whether of guilty or not-guilty pleas (QIV 1987/9, QIV 1987/9), despite below-median not-guilty plea rates (QII 1987/9) and average remand rates (25.2 per cent 1987, 17.2 per cent 1989). This delay may have accounted for the high rates of judicial discharge pre-empanelment (QIV 1989) and directed acquittals (QIV 1989). There was variation between the years for jury acquittals (QI 1987, QIII 1989) but consistent QII rates of majority verdict on conviction (8 per cent 1987, 7.4 per cent 1989). For defendants pleading guilty custodial sentence rates were low (QI 1987/9) but inconsistent for those convicted at trial (QIV 1987, QI 1989).

Can one however point to any distinguishing features which, at least as tendency or weak generalization, distinguish rural Crown Court justice from its urban counterparts – apart from their low case-loads? Certainly there is little to be risked about the acquittal rates, whether of judges or juries – unless one groups them together. However one can point out one such tendency: judges in these courts tend towards a lower rate of custodial sentence for those pleading guilty (QI, QII). The other characteristic is perhaps surprising because it concerns neither judges nor juries, but rural defendants. They tend to plead not guilty more frequently (QIV, QIII), and hereby hangs a conclusion. We have already seen that the non-risk-taking guilty pleaders fare relatively leniently. But it can be argued that the not-guilty pleaders also fare relatively well, or to be pedantic, relatively not badly. Two measures are presented here: 'unsuccessful trials' (table 4.13), that is all acquittals, whether by discharge, direction or jury, of not-guilty pleas; and 'unsuccessful prosecutions', that is such acquittals as a percentage of all cases, guilty plea or not-guilty plea, in the system (table 4.14). It can be seen that, although the spread is quite wide, only Dorchester features in Quartile I, and in table 4.14 Quartile IV is dominated by these rural courts, and none feature in Quartile I.

Table 4.13 *'Unsuccessful' trials % all acquittals of N-G pleas (bailed defendants, 60 courts)*

1987			1989		
QI	20.5	*Portsmouth*	QI	(28.6)	Salisbury
	37.0	Dorchester		42.2	Dorchester
QII	40.0	Taunton	QII	49.3	Newport (IoW)
	42.6	Caernarfon			
	42.7	Carmarthen		52.0	Barnstaple
	44.0	Newport (IoW)			
M	45.0	*Lincoln*	M	53.5	Caernarfon
QIII	46.3	Barnstaple	QIII	(55.0)	Welshpool
				55.7	Bodmin-Truro
QIV	57.5	Bodmin-Truro	QIV	67.3	Carmarthen
	61.5	Haverfordwest		67.6	Taunton
	65.8	*Doncaster*		68.9	*Burnley*
Range	45.3			40.3	
Rural	24.5			39.0	

Table 4.14 *'Unsuccessful' prosecutions % (all acquittals of GP and NGP) (bailed defendants, 62 courts)*

1987			1989		
QI	4.4	*Worcester-Hereford*	QI	5.0	*Durham*
QII	9.3	Taunton	QII	10.6	Salisbury
M	11.3	*Bolton*	M	14.0	Haverfordwest
QIII	12.6	Caernarfon	QIII	14.9	Bodmin-Truro
	15.0	Barnstaple			
QIV	18.1	Bodmin-Truro	QIV	17.8	Barnstaple
				18.0	Taunton
	20.3	Carmarthen		18.1	Caernarfon
	21.0	Dorchester		19.9	Newport (IoW)
	21.8	Newport (IoW)		20.5	Welshpool
	26.2	Haverfordwest		21.0	Dorchester
	31.0	Salisbury		25.0	Carmarthen
Range	26.6			20.0	
Rural	21.7			14.4	

5

The Magistrate in a Rural Area with particular reference to Courts in West Wales

MARGARET GWYNNE LLOYD

Historical Background

The magistrate has been part of the rural scene for centuries, even though the exact date of the first appearance of the justice of the peace may be open to dispute among historians. Maitland in his *Constitutional History* and Beard in his *Office of the Justice of the Peace* regard the Stat. 34, Ed. III, Cap. 1 as the starting-point, but other historians, notably Putnam,[1] have unearthed evidence which suggests that this statute gave legal sanction to an institution which already had proved its worth.

Justices themselves, however, by celebrating their sexcentury in 1961, look upon the Justices of the Peace Act of 1361, as their 'birth certificate'.[2] The Act stipulated:

> In every county of England shall be assigned for the keeping of the peace, one lord and with him three or four of the most worthy in the county, with some learned in the law, and they shall have power to restrain the offenders, rioters and all other barrators [exciters of quarrels] and to pursue, arrest, take and chastise them according to their trespass and offence . . . and to take and arrest all those that they may by indictment, or by suspicion, and to put them in prison . . . and

[1] B. H. Putnam, 'The transformation of the Keepers of the Peace into the Justices of the Peace', *Transactions of the Royal Historical Society*, 4th Series, 12 (1929).

[2] E. Milton, *The English Magistracy* (London, 1967), 4.

> also to hear and determine at the King's Suit all manner of felonies and trespasses done in the same county, according to the laws and customs aforesaid.[3]

If the exact origins of the magistrating in England have proved elusive, a similar problem has also been encountered in determining the date of the appointment of the first justices in Wales. The Act of 27 Hen. VIII, c. 5, entitled 'An Act for making of Justices in Wales', stated 'that one order of ministering of his Laws should be had, observed and used in the same way as in other places of this Realm of England had and used'. Justices in the counties of Chester, Flint, Anglesey, Caernarfon, Merioneth, Cardigan, Carmarthen, Pembroke and Glamorgan were to have the same power and authority as justices in England. Some historians have held that justices of the peace appeared quickly after the 1536 Act, but more recent scholarship maintains that justices did not appear in Wales for some years after the Act 27, Hen. VIII, c. 5 which first authorized their appointment. Phillips[4] states that the first definite pieces of evidence that justices of the peace were acting in Wales relate to October 1541 and that there is 'no reason to believe that their appointment was other than recent'.

As in England in the fourteenth century, so in Wales by the Act of Union (1536–41) in the sixteenth century, the salient features were established of a lay and local institution which were to continue until the present day. It is not the purpose of this paper to trace the many vicissitudes of the magistracy in rural Wales during the past four centuries, except to say that up until the beginning of the twentieth century, the magistracy and the landed gentry were practically synonymous, and that members of the same families were to be found on the county benches year after year.

It was the twentieth century that broke this almost monopolistic hold of the gentry on the administration of rural justice. The first significant weakening of the centuries–old grip was brought about in 1906 by the abolition of the property qualification for country magistrates (Justices of the Peace Act). In 1911, came the report of the Royal Commission on the Selection of Justices of the Peace;[5] this paved the way for the appointment of men of all social classes to local benches, both urban and rural. With the dismantling of

[3] J. H. Lewis, 'The Justice of the Peace in Wales', *Transactions of the Honourable Society of Cymmrodorion* (1943–4), 120–32.

[4] J. R. S. Phillips, *The Justices of the Peace in Wales and Monmouthshire, 1541–1689* (Cardiff, 1975).

[5] *Royal Commission on the Selection of Justices of the Peace*, Cd 5250 (London, 1910).

property and class restrictions, there remained, in law, only the sex disqualification; the all-male bench was to disappear for ever by the passing of the 1919 Sex Disqualification (Removal) Act.

It is not to be assumed that the widening of the field of selection of magistrates received unanimous and universal approval. Writing in 1926, H. M. Vaughan, High Sheriff of Cardiganshire from 1916 to 1917, lamented the changing composition of the county benches. They have been filled, he says, 'with ambitious members from a different social stratum . . . the majority on these Benches is nowadays usually composed of ex-officio members . . . and of successful tradesmen and profiteers, with a small sprinkling of farmers.'[6] A misogynist, he could not even bring himself to mention the recent appointment of women justices to the county benches of Cardiganshire, Pembrokeshire and Carmarthenshire.

Another big shake-up in the magisterial system took place in the years following the termination of hostilities in 1945. A Royal Commission was set up in 1946 and reported in 1948.[7] Almost all its majority recommendations were accepted and were incorporated in the 1949 Justices of the Peace Act. This Act tightened up on the appointment of magistrates by imposing certain conditions regarding the physical fitness of candidates (e.g., blindness was considered to be an absolute ban, and deafness, while being a less detectable infirmity, was also considered to be a very serious defect). The 1949 Act also recommended that amateur magistrates should be given some training. At this time, too, many rural benches had too many magistrates; drastic pruning took place by introducing a compulsory retiring age of seventy-five, by not replacing much of the national wastage and by removing those who were not carrying out their duties either through ill health or through lack of commitment from the Active List to the Supplemental List (created in 1941).

More changes were to follow in the 1960s. In 1966 all new magistrates were obliged to give an undertaking that they would complete a prescribed course of training. The 1968 Justices of the Peace Act abolished, apart from one or two named exceptions, ex-officio justices (chairmen of urban and rural district councils and mayors), thus confining the office of justice of the peace to persons selected and subsequently trained for it. This Act further reduced the retiring age – magistrates were now to be transferred to the Supplemental List on reaching the age of seventy, and the Act gave legal sanction to the payment of travelling, subsistence and financial loss allowances.

[6] H. M. Vaughan, *The South Wales Squires* (Carmarthen, 1988 [1926]).

[7] *Royal Commission on Justices of the Peace*, Cmd 7463 (London, 1948).

The Present-day Composition of a Rural Bench in West Wales

The aim of all these changes has been to democratize the magistracy, which, for so many centuries, had been the almost exclusive preserve of the landed gentry, and to make the bench a balanced reflection of the local community it serves.

This question of 'balance' has been described in the following terms: 'each Bench should be a microcosm of the local community and this amounts to seeing that in every Petty Sessional Division there are at least some justices from each of the principal social and political groups in the area and that the Bench is not dominated by any one group.'[8]

The same thinking was confirmed and reiterated as recently as 1988 by the Lord Chancellor's Department.[9]

> The magistracy is open to all eligible persons regardless of race, religion, colour, social class, sex or political opinion. These factors have no part to play in determining personal suitability for appointment. But second only to the requirement that candidates must be personally suitable is the desirability that each bench should include men and women from all backgrounds and walks of life throughout the petty session area and thereby broadly reflect the local community.

It is pertinent to ask if small rural benches achieve a balance in terms of age, occupation, gender and politics which reflects the broad spectrum of opinion that exists in the community at large. My own bench, Gogledd Preseli, consists of eleven members (six men, five women), with the average age of the bench being fifty-eight. All members are or have been connected with farming or with teaching. There are some good reasons for the presence of teachers and farmers on a rural bench. Farming is the major industry, and there is a large and excellent pool of teachers on which to draw. Farmers can, if they wish, often organize their work to fit in with court duties, and teachers, up until the introduction of the Local Management of Schools, have had time off generous enough to make room for such activities. By no stretch of the imagination, however, can such a bench be said to reflect the local community. It may be that it is asking the impossible for very small benches to be even broadly representative of their petty session division, but there are dangers when magistrates are drawn from just two occupations.

It is not that one social/occupational class would blatantly

[8] T. Skyrme, *The Changing Image of the Magistracy* (London, 1979), 62–3.

[9] Lord Chancellor's Department, 'The qualities looked for in a Justice of the Peace', *The Magistrate*, 44, 5 (1988), 78.

dominate another for its own ends, as in the oft-quoted example of the local landowner fiercely punishing the poacher. It is rather that a bench overdependent on one or two occupations, with their associated social background, may not have the necessary familiarity with the 'nuts and bolts' of ordinary people's lives.[10] A greater diversity of experience, social and educational background and personality is particularly important when it comes to dealing with cases which are either unusual or exceptional.

Nor is it a question of potential bias being caused by proprietary or pecuniary interest. Gone, hopefully for ever, is the sort of scandal that involved the Aberaeron justices in 1946 in the case of *James* v. *Lewis* (*Times*, 12 December 1946). The clerk to the Aberaeron bench was also the local Food Executive Officer and was charged with making a false statement in an application for a licence to slaughter a pig. The Aberaeron magistrates heard the case themselves and dismissed the charge at the end of the prosecution case. The divisional court strongly criticized all involved for not transferring the case to another court or for not committing for trial. The divisional court remitted the case and ordered that the justices and the clerk be reported to the Lord Chancellor and Law Society respectively.[11]

The issue is rather that both teachers and farmers face subtle potential problems in the exercise of their duties. Teachers would be the first to acknowledge that their connection with a school, particularly if the catchment area of that school is practically coterminous with the Petty Sessional Division (PSD), brings them into frequent conflict with their role as a magistrate. It is often inappropriate for them to sit on a case involving a recent pupil if his/her general conduct has to be considered by the court. It is also possible that a former pupil might claim bias for some time after leaving school, especially if he/she had a stormy school career. Again, it has been suggested that a school teacher employed by the county council should not sit on a truancy case concerning another school run by the same county council.[12]

The possibility of bias arising through analogous interests is something that also faces farmers. Offences involving agricultural pollution is a case in point. Furthermore the farming community is one of the most stable of all social classes and is well blessed with long, well-established and extensive local connections. Farmers have an unrivalled knowledge of their PSD, and local knowledge is

[10] E. Burney, *Magistrate, Court and Community* (London, 1979), 222.

[11] R. D. S. Stevens, *Bias and Impartiality in Magistrates' Courts* (Chichester, 1952), 10.

[12] Ibid., 83.

recognized to be 'one of the great strengths of the lay magistracy and perhaps its chief justification'.[13] Nevertheless, a recent study of magistrates' courts warns of the reverse side to this coin.[14] Many defendants prefer to be tried before an anonymous bench which they believe would be more impartial.

Rural magistrates would strongly dispute any suggestion that impartiality can be an attribute only of anonymity. Yet there is perhaps a grain of truth in the assertion that rural courts have to be extra vigilant not to give any impression of bias in their dealings with defendants who are drawn from the same tightly knit communities.

Perhaps the most insidious difficulty of all that faces a homogeneous bench with a narrow social composition is that its decision-making could become too bland and comfortable. 'The very *raison d'être* of the magistracy rests on the principle that justice can be administered by groups of laymen whose idiosyncracies and prejudices will be neutralised and absorbed in deliberation with others from different backgrounds.'[15] When a bench is deprived of a wide and varied spectrum of values and opinions, could it be in danger of losing its *raison d'être*?

The Size of a Rural Bench

Rural benches are unlikely to suffer the disadvantages of being too large; they are far more likely to suffer the disadvantages of being too small. In a document entitled 'The size of benches',[16] the Lord Chancellor's Department and the Home Office suggested that a bench of fewer than twelve magistrates is likely to be too small to continue as a separate unit for the efficient and effective administration of justice. Three main reasons were put forward to support this point of view. Firstly, a bench with fewer than twelve justices is unlikely to be adequately balanced in such matters as age, sex, occupational and social background, location of residence and political affiliations (if any). This matter has already been discussed and found to contain an element of truth. Secondly, if a bench is very small, there may not be enough business to permit each justice to get enough experience. This question will be examined later when the numbers and duration of sittings and the workload of a rural bench

[13] D. Faulkner, 'Crime and the courts', *The Magistrate*, 43, 11 (1957), 207.

[14] J. W. Raine, *Local Justice: Ideals and Realities* (Edinburgh, 1989), 82.

[15] J. Baldwin, 'The social composition of the magistracy', *British Journal of Criminology*, 16 (1976), 171–4.

[16] Home Office, Lord Chancellor's Department, 'The size of benches', *The Magistrate*, 43, 8 (1986), 118–21.

will be analysed in some detail. Thirdly, the document states that with benches of fewer than twelve justices, there is unlikely to be adequate opportunity for the regular introduction of new blood. On my own bench, for example, there has been one new appointment in the last five years, and five new appointments in the last ten years. So again there is an element of truth in this assertion.

In his response to proposals to amalgamate two small rural benches in North Yorkshire, one being a bench of seven justices, the other being a bench of ten, Professor I. R. Scott warns against a too rigorous application of the 'small' bench number of twelve, particularly in far-flung rural areas. He states that there is no such thing as an optimum PSD size, and that the notion that a bench of less than twelve must necessarily be rather 'incestuous' is frequently no more than an argument to isolate a case for amalgamation of Divisions based on grounds of administrative economy. Many factors, he concludes, must be considered, and it is only on the balance of the advantages and disadvantages of these that rural benches should be amalgamated. In the case of the two small North Yorkshire benches, Professor Scott finally comes down in favour of amalgamation which, as far as the magistrates are concerned, would bring them the advantages of a more balanced bench and increased experience.[17]

Professor Scott does not address the specific question of how to ensure the regular introduction of new blood. Burney has suggested that this problem could be overcome by giving serious consideration to limiting the tenure of office of magistrate to ten years at a time.[18] Raine also considers this possibility, and while recognizing that it might seem wasteful to release magistrates after a ten-year service, having trained them and developed their expertise, he comes to the conclusion that 'on balance, the advantages to local justice of restricted tenure would seem to outweigh the disadvantages.'[19]

This is a proposal which would have a mixed reception from rural magistrates. It is not that they are opposed to the introduction of new blood by means of a restricted tenure of office, but, given the number and duration of court sittings, and the size and nature of their workload, they feel that it takes almost ten years to get to know the job, for their experience is slow to accumulate. They would argue that such a measure could be considered only after a review of the number and duration of court sittings of their Divisions

[17] I. R. Scott, *Report of Local Inquiry into North Yorkshire Magistrates' Courts. Committee's Proposal to Amalgamate the Petty Session Divisions of Hang East and Hang West* (Leeds, 1989).

[18] Burney, op. cit., 224.

[19] Raine, op. cit., 188.

in relation to the case load involved, in order to ensure that there are sufficient magistrates whose experience has covered a wide range of offences and sentences, available to take the chair and to be effective 'wingers'.

Number and Duration of Court Sittings

The document 'The size of benches' also contains some guidelines as to the number and duration of court sittings. 'The Lord Chancellor takes the view', the document states, 'that each justice should sit at least 26 times a year if he or she is to have adequate experience.' Successive Lord Chancellors have held the same view. Lord Hailsham,[20] in his presidential address to the annual general meeting of the Magistrates' Association in 1984, emphasized that twenty-six sittings per year constituted a minimum requirement and that thirty to thirty-five half-day sittings would represent a more realistic figure in order for magistrates to acquire the necessary experience. The document goes on to say that for each magistrate to achieve this number of sittings, there should be in each PSD at least 134 planned sittings a year – two adult courts each week (104 a year), one juvenile court and one domestic court each month (twelve a year respectively) and a licensing court every other month (six a year).

Looking at the 1990 list of planned court sittings for my Division, the adult court sittings, which also include licensing sessions, amount to seventy-two. This Division does not have its own domestic or juvenile courts, but has a joint domestic panel and a joint juvenile panel with a neighbouring Division. Both the domestic court and the juvenile court sit twice a month.[21]

How does this list of planned court sittings work out for an individual magistrate? The following is my personal experience. In 1990 my name appeared on the adult and licensing rota 25 times; this number of planned sittings was achieved by being one of four magistrates – a most unsatisfactory number – on fifteen occasions. As a member of the domestic panel, I was listed to sit four times in 1990. In these circumstances one can hardly claim to have accumulated experience of sufficient breadth of depth in either the adult court or in the domestic court.

In addition to the number of court sittings, the Lord Chancellor's

[20] Lord Hailsham, presidential address delivered to the annual general meeting of the Magistrates' Association in October 1984, *The Magistrate*, 41, 1 (1985), 2–4.

[21] L. G. Henshaw notes a similar pattern of planned court sittings in most of the benches in Powys, *The Governance and Organisation of the Magistrates' Courts Services* (unpublished PhD thesis for the University of Wales), 289–90.

Department and the Home Office formulated, in their joint circular, criteria relating to the duration of court sittings. While recognizing that much depends on local circumstances, it is suggested that any bench, which in respect of normal scheduled courts sits on average for less than, say, two hours on each sitting day, should consider the feasibility and usefulness of sitting for longer sessions but on fewer days. It must be pointed out, however, when court sittings are scheduled, as in our case, for once a fortnight, to reduce this frequency could have serious implications. It could increase the delays which hinder the progress of cases through the criminal justice process. Adjournment, for example, would be for a minimum of three or even four weeks; 'first call' and 'advanced disclosure' procedures would also mean that cases would be spread out over a longer period of time. The joint circular goes on to say that any such bench which sees no scope for changing its sitting pattern should be regarded as prima facie a candidate for amalgamation.

The annual number of sitting hours recorded for the adult courts and licensing sessions in our PSD totalled 202 hours, an average of 2.8 hours per court sitting, based on seventy-two scheduled court sittings per year.[22] The joint document makes the point that short court sittings are bound to be costly in terms of use of accommodation and in the demands they make on the police, the Crown Prosecution Service and on the magistrates' clerks. But to my mind, it is of equal concern that a small number of sittings of short duration is likely to have an adverse effect on the quality of experience a rural magistrate accumulates over the years. It is therefore proposed to consider in some detail the size and nature of this workload.

Workload in terms of Offences

Invaluable information regarding the workload of Petty Sessional Divisions is contained in volume 5 of the *Criminal Statistics* published annually by the Home Office.[23] Dyfed, the Commissioners of the Peace area, is mainly rural in character, but there are some urban centres, clustered in Llanelli, Carmarthen South, Cleddau, Dinefwr and South Pembrokeshire. The remaining Divisions in Dyfed, Ceredigion Ganol, Gogledd Ceredigion, De Ceredigion, Carmarthen North and Gogledd Preseli, cover the more sparsely populated areas. Table 5.1, which shows the number of persons proceeded against in all the Dyfed PSDs, by offence type, gives a good

[22] Statistics supplied by the clerk to the Dyfed Magistrates' Courts Committee.

[23] Home Office, *Criminal Statistics, England and Wales. Supplementary Tables*, vol. 5, Annual Reports (London, Government Statistical Service).

Table 5.1 *Persons proceeded against at magistrates' courts by petty sessional division and offence type, 1987 and 1988*

Petty sessional division	Total all offences		Indictable		Summary non-motoring		Summary motoring	
	1987	1988	1987	1988	1987	1988	1987	1988
Llanelli	2672	2204	710	703	880	837	1082	664
Ceredigion Ganol	396	456	78	107	131	189	187	160
Gogledd Ceredigion	894	1015	242	234	259	318	393	463
De Ceredigion	440	438	124	68	161	163	155	207
Carmarthen North	166	197	30	39	36	81	94	77
Carmarthen South	1442	1387	310	291	322	331	810	765
Cleddau	1705	1604	437	429	524	520	744	655
Dinefwr	1093	774	247	213	390	314	456	247
Gogledd Preseli	361	354	54	59	100	134	207	161
South Pembrokeshire	1526	1574	367	383	447	402	712	789

Source: *Criminal Statistics, England and Wales, supplementary tables*, vol. 5, 1987 and 1988.

idea of the range of workloads undertaken within a predominantly rural Commission of the Peace area. The figures in table 5.1 indicate quite clearly the small size of the workload of PSDs in the more rural areas. Gogledd Preseli, my own PSD, is not unexpectedly at the lower end of the scale.

Not only is it illuminating to establish the size of the workload, but also its composition in terms of gravity of offence. Table 5.2 analyses in more detail the indictable offences which have been dealt with by the Gogledd Preseli bench, in 1986, 1987 and 1988. The statistics in table 5.2, sketching the crime profile of our PSD, indicate the relative absence of very serious crime, a state of affairs that magistrates sitting on busy inner-city benches would view with deep envy. It is our fervent hope that the law-abiding ethos of rural west Wales, as suggested by these statistics, will remain undiminished in the years ahead. But when the occasional serious crime does present itself, could we magistrates be in danger of either over- or underreaction? Not having experience of the range of gravity, for example, in sexual offences, robbery, football hooliganism or troublesome acid house parties, how are we to establish the degree of seriousness when an isolated case comes before us? Even in motoring offences, which constitute the bulk of our work, because there is no motorway in our area, motoring offences associated with the upper range of

Table 5.2 *Persons sentenced in Gogledd Preseli for indictable offences by offence group*

	1986	1987	1988
Total indictable offences	11	40	35
Violence against the person	4	6	3
Sexual offences	–	–	–
Burglary	1	3	7
Robbery	–	–	–
Theft and handling	3	4	10
Fraud and forgery	–	3	–
Criminal damage	1	2	3
Drug offences	–	4	5
Other indictable non-motoring	1	10	2
Indictable motoring	1	8	5

Source: *Criminal Statistics*, England and Wales, supplementary tables, volume 5, 1986, 1987, 1988

excessive speeds, multiple accidents, etc., do not find their way into our lists. To be constantly aware of the whole range of gravity in serious offences requires regular and structured training in these matters and a new warp of gaining wide and practical experience. These issues will be considered later.

Workload in terms of Sentences

An analysis of bench workload from the point of view of the way in which cases are disposed of throws further light on the limited experience of some rural magistrates. Table 5.3 gives the number of persons found guilty of indictable offences and the sentences given by the Gogledd Preseli, Cleddau and South Pembrokeshire PSDs, all served by the same clerkship. Figures for the three PSDs are given for comparative purposes.

Since Gogledd Preseli does not have its own juvenile court, there are no separate figures showing the use of young offender institutions and care orders. Neither are there any attendance centre orders for any of the Divisions in the former county of Pembrokeshire because there is no attendance centre available in the area. During 1987 and 1988, the most frequent disposal used by the Gogledd Preseli bench, as indeed by any other bench, was the fine. Other disposals were relatively infrequently used – probation nine times in two years, community service order five times in two years, fully suspended prison sentence on four occasions in the same period of time, and one immediate custodial sentence in two years.

The total bench experience in imposing these sentences and in establishing the correct tariff could not be described as being extensive, and the experience of each individual magistrate would be even more diluted. So, with, for example, only five community service orders being imposed in two years, how do we arrive at gauging the correct number of hours? By accepting implicitly the recommendation of the probation officer? In this context, the guidelines relating to community service order hours, which are in the process of being worked out by the Magistrates' Association, will be invaluable, as indeed have been the Association's other guidelines on sentences relating to motoring and non-motoring offences.

There are, however, other sentencing options which have not been used at all. According to the unpublished records kept by the clerk to the magistrates, disposals under the mental health legislation have never been called into operation by the Gogledd Preseli bench since it first came into an amalgamated being in 1986. This is a serious gap in our experience.

The limited experience of a small rural bench in terms of offences and sentences was to some extent offset in the past by regular attendance at a Crown Court. Sitting in the Crown Court was invaluable in accumulating knowledge of the upper range of serious offences and the sort of sentences such offences would attract. This helped to put our own work into better perspective. It also provided excellent opportunities to see how professional judges sifted evidence, structured a sentencing decision and controlled their courts. But since 1986, shortage of funds has put a stop to magistrates attending a Crown Court, except when required for appeals. This curtailment is to be regretted, for it denies magistrates a chance to benefit from a much-needed and much-appreciated association with another branch of the judiciary.

It could well be argued that in spite of limited experience, rural benches are meeting the criminal justice needs of their areas and that appeals against their sentences and decisions are relatively few.[24] This may well be so. But I would suggest that limited

[24] Although many factors influence both prosecution and defence in deciding whether or not to appeal against sentences and decisions of magistrates, the number of such appeals can be taken as an indication that the sentencing policy of a particular bench is not too out of line with what is expected. Between July 1986 and September 1990, there were from the Gogledd Preseli bench decisions and sentences, 11 appeals on criminal matters and one appeal on a licensing matter. In the words of the clerk to the Pembrokeshire magistrates, this was a very low rating on the 'Richter Scale'.

Table 5.3 *Persons found guilty on indictable offences and sentences given*

Year	PSD	Total guilty	Committed for sentence	Absolute discharge or conditional discharge	Probation or supervision	Fine	Community service order	Attendance centre	Detention centre	Care	Fully suspended sentence	Partly suspended sentence	Youth custody	Unsuspended sentence	Otherwise dealt with
1987	Gogledd Preseli	40	0	2	4	27	4	0	0	0	1	0	0	0	2
	Cleddau	299	4	66	47	134	20	0	1	1	8	1	2	8	7
	South Pembrokeshire	258	4	22	29	149	36	0	2	1	4	0	2	2	7
	Total	597	8	90	80	310	60	0	3	2	13	1	4	10	16
									YOI				YOI		
1988	Gogledd Preseli	35	0	7	5	17	1	0	0	0	3	0	0	1	1
	Cleddau	274	5	58	43	112	18	0	16	1	7	2	0	5	7
	South Pembrokeshire	234	4	13	21	121	28	0	14	1	14	0	0	12	6
	Total	543	9	78	69	250	47	0	30	2	24	2	0	18	14

Source: *Criminal Statistics*, England and Wales, supplementary tables, vol. 5, 1987 and 1988

experience can undermine the self-confidence and self-assurance of rural magistrates *vis-à-vis* other agencies in the court room, and these qualities are going to be all-important in the correct control of their courts in the future.

The Control of the Court

In one sense, control of the court means upholding the dignity of the court in the face of contempt or misbehaviour. It is not this aspect I wish to discuss but the effectiveness of control of the conduct of the court by magistrates in the face of the increased power and influence of other professions – justices' clerks, the Crown Prosecution Service and social workers. 'Between the welfare and legal professions, the lay justice shrinks in status.'[25] For lay justices in rural areas whose experience is limited through no fault of their own, it is a doubly difficult task to pit themselves against the strongly professional and career-minded Crown Prosecution Service, justices' clerks, police, forensic services, probation and prison services and defence lawyers. Yet when the priorities and aspirations of the executive and other agencies are at variance with those of the court, the lay justice must ensure that those of the court take precedence. It requires considerable self-confidence, self-assurance and skill on the part of the lay magistrate to know exactly when to question in open court any failures in the judicial process. Why did it take so long to bring the case? Why cannot the case proceed now? Why is it necessary to delay by two weeks, a month? Why cannot we offer an earlier date for trial? Why did the Crown Prosecution Service take it on themselves to send only one prosecution rather than two, thus effectively cancelling a court without giving magistrates any foreknowledge and causing three magistrates to be superfluous to the day's needs? Questions such as these need to be asked in appropriate circumstances if lay magistrates are going to maintain effective control of court proceedings.

Inroads into the lay control of the courts through professional intervention can occur on yet another front. This is in the delicate balance of the relationship between clerk and magistrate. The role of the justices' clerk in the courtroom has long given rise to debate and comment. So often proceedings seem to be conducted as a professional interchange between Crown Prosecution Service, defence lawyers and the clerk rather than between defendant and the magistrates. Again, there has been concern that clerks might be influencing magistrates unduly in the retiring room. Back in 1952,

[25] Burney, op. cit., 215.

Lord Goddard commented in the Court of Appeal that the decision of the court must be the decision of the justices, and not that of the justices and their clerk, and that if the clerk retires with the justices as a matter of course, it is inevitable that the impression will be given that he may influence the justices as to the decision or sentence, or both.[26] More recently, in February 1989, a decision of the Queen's Bench Division ruled that not only should a clerk not retire with his justices as a matter of course, but that whenever justices retiring to consider a matter wished their clerk to accompany them to give advice, their request to him to do so should be made clearly and in open court. 'Justices should be concerned with the appearance of justice as much as with justice itself.'[27]

Yet another aspect of court proceedings where clerks sometimes seem to be maintaining an unnecessarily high profile is in the pronouncements of sentence. So frequently the clerk repeats and/or elaborates what the lay chairperson has said. It may well be, for example, that in the case of a community service order or a probation order the chairperson of a rural bench may not have had a great deal of experience in explaining in simple everyday language to the defendant what these orders entail, but this is a matter of training and not of role, and the clerk should not assume to himself the role of the lay chairperson.

These encroachments into the lay magistrates' control of court proceedings are largely a consequence of the increasing professionalization of local justice, a trend which has been gathering momentum during the last decade.[28] The lay control of the small rural bench has been made particularly vulnerable by these developments. The prospect of even more professionalization coupled with even more centralization as envisaged by the report of the Le Vay Scrutiny[29] is, from the point of view of rural justice and lay justice, deeply worrying.

If the Le Vay proposals are adopted, even in a modified form, the administration of magistrates' courts will be run as a national service and will be a central government responsibility. Le Vay goes to great lengths to emphasize that the lay magistracy will remain independent and will continue to deliver local justice in local courts. Nevertheless, the new-style court managers will, in the last analysis, be answerable to the Home Office for efficiency and cash-control

26 *R.* v. *East Kerrier Justices ex parte Mundy* [1952] 2 QB 719, 2 All ER 144 116 JP 339.

27 *R.* v. *Eccles Justices, ex parte Fitzpatrick* [1989] 153 JP 470, [1989] NLJR 9435, DC.

28 *Times*, 28 February 1989.

29 Home Office, *A Report of a Scrutiny*, 2 vols. (London, 1989).

targets. There is considerable unease that the highly professional court clerk/manager, with one eye on his career in a centralized administration, will put pressure on lay magistrates to conform to efficiency and management norms set by the executive.

In spite of repeated assurances from Home Office officials, there are unallayed fears that the independence of the lay magistracy will be under serious threat in the future. The Home Office, which already has direct control over the police, the probation and prison services, will, with a centralized administration of magistrates' courts within its sphere of influence, have completely outflanked the lay magistracy. For lay magistrates to assert the independence granted to them by Parliament, within the confines of a rural courtroom, surrounded by powerful agencies all answerable to one gigantic department of central government, headed by the Home Secretary, is a daunting prospect. This is why magistrates, both rural and urban, would prefer to have the administration of their courts – if it has to be centralized – placed with that of the Crown Courts in the ambit of the Lord Chancellor's Department.

In view of all these factors, rural magistrates need, as a matter of urgency, to consider how best to overcome the twin disadvantages of limited experience and declining relative status. In order to re-establish their central position as independent arbiters of conflicting claims, aims, opinions and issues, there must be fresh thought given to designing training programmes which will meet their specific needs and to increasing their individual workloads.

Training

Training has long been regarded as the panacea for helping magistrates to perform their duties in the most efficient and competent manner. Courses, conferences, lectures and sentencing exercises have been devised in order to promote instruction in the law, administration of justice and sentencing options. A solid foundation of basic training for every magistrate, and the opportunity for all at regular intervals to refresh their knowledge and re-evaluate the quality of the work they do, have been the cornerstones of these programmes.

It may be argued, however, that in the past there has been too much emphasis on extending the legal knowledge of magistrates. 'In this context perhaps the problem is that most training of magistrates lies in the hands of justices' clerks to senior magistrates who, of course, have themselves previously been trained by justices' clerks.'[30] Another commentator has written, 'Clerks may be good

[30] Raine, op. cit., 200.

in law and procedure, but they are not really interested in the *decision* and the decision-making process.'[31] Yet this is the very area in which magistrates need help: to analyse the issues, to present reasons and to structure decisions. Training therefore should be much more broadly based and should include subjects such as structured decision-making, evaluating evidence and witnesses, examining group dynamics and improving skills in pronouncing sentences, all of which should supplement the usual diet of new legislation, rules of evidence and sentencing exercises conducted in groups too large to be useful. Experts other than justices' clerks should therefore also be involved in the training of magistrates.

In support of this approach, Raine and Burney further argue that training should never attempt to create a bench whose knowledge of the law matches that of professional lawyers – whether they be clerks, crown prosecutors or defence solicitors. It is the 'lay status' of the magistracy that gives it its distinctive character and identity. If magistrates 'cease to represent a genuinely lay view and become half-baked professionals . . . they will miss the essence of their role, the common touch.'[32] 'Magistrates need to be "street-wise" rather than case-wise.'[33]

Not only is there a danger that magistrates' training is orientated too much towards legislation, there is also a suspicion that magistrates in rural areas do not have sufficient opportunities to re-evaluate the quality of their work. During the first nine months of 1990, for example, nothing had been arranged by the Dyfed Magistrates' Courts Committee for magistrates who have long since completed their basic training, but who have not reached the stage of taking the chair. The highly appreciated and successful Aberystwyth biennial residential training conference, which had been held regularly since 1958 and which should have taken place in April 1990, was not arranged, because, it was asserted, of lack of funds.

Future training programmes have thus to steer between the Scylla and Charybdis of too little training and too much of the wrong sort. They will need to concentrate on increasing skills in decision-making and on confirming magistrates in their lay status and common sense, and to draw on experts from disciplines other than the legal profession in order to broaden the spectrum of instruction.

[31] A. Samuels, 'The attitude of magistrates to training: a critical comment', *The Magistrate*, 45, 9 (1989), 154.

[32] Burney, op. cit., 216.

[33] Raine, op. cit., 199.

Increasing the Experience of Rural Magistrates

The point has already been made that magistrates assigned to small rural benches such as Gogledd Preseli sit too infrequently, for too few hours, and thus, through no fault of their own, are unable to gain sufficient experience of the range and gravity of offences and of the range of sentencing options. While wishing to avoid the other extreme of sitting too often and of becoming almost full-time and 'case-hardened', there must be a model which would serve the criminal justice needs of a rural area better than the present set-up.

In the area of the former county of Pembrokeshire, there are now three PSDs: Cleddau, South Pembrokeshire and Gogledd Preseli. The total area measures some 452 square miles, with an estimated 1990 population of some 70,000. There is considerable disparity in the workload of these three Divisions, with magistrates in Cleddau having to shoulder the heaviest workload.[34] Table 5.4 gives the details.

Table 5.4

1989	Cleddau	South Pembrokeshire	Gogledd Preseli
Total sitting hours	1425	535	209
Total number of cases dealt with	2824	909	431

Source: Dyfed Magistrates' Courts Committee: Court Houses Report 1990.[34]

For purposes of comparison, table 5.5 shows the total sitting hours and total number of cases dealt with by the combined three Pembrokeshire PSDs and by the Llanelli PSD, the most urban area in Dyfed, in 1989.

If the three Pembrokeshire Divisions were to be amalgamated, there would be some seventy-seven magistrates available to share the total sitting hours and total numbers of cases dealt with. There are on the Llanelli bench some forty-seven magistrates. A simple arithmetical calculation indicates that each of the Pembrokeshire magistrates – after amalgamation – would still have a higher workload and would still sit for fewer hours than his colleague on the Llanelli bench.

Looked at from a slightly different angle, an amalgamated

[34] Dyfed Magistrates' Courts Committee, Court Houses Report, unpublished report to Dyfed County Council (1990).

Table 5.5

1989	The combined three Pembrokeshire PSDs	Llanelli
Total hours per annum	2169	1474
Total number of cases dealt with	4164	3465

Source: Dyfed Magistrates' Court Committee: Court Houses Report, 1990

Pembrokeshire Division of seventy-seven magistrates would be one magistrate per 912 head of population. In the rural Divisions of North Yorkshire studied by Professor Scott,[35] the highest ratio of magistrates to population was one per 1,510 population, and the lowest ratio was one magistrate to 3,073 head of population.

So, if one considers the ratio of magistrates to population on the size of the workload, an amalgamated Pembrokeshire Division would still have an abundance of justices to fulfil the criminal justice needs of the area. Indeed, it has even been suggested that the number of Pembrokeshire magistrates should be reduced from seventy-seven to fifty in order to ensure a sufficient and varied experience for each individual magistrate – in terms of offences and sentences.

Whenever the amalgamation of Divisions is proposed, the whole question of how local local justice should be is debated anew. There was a time when many more Divisions existed than at present. For example, up to 1954, Cilgennan, Castlemartin, Dungleddy, Roose, the boroughs of Haverfordwest, Pembroke and Tenby all had their own PSDs. In 1954, however, the Home Secretary, Mr Gwilym Lloyd George, signed a Statutory Instrument which abolished these small benches and created the new Division of Cemaes, Haverfordwest, Narbeth, Pembroke and Tenby.[36] In 1984, Mr Leon Brittan signed a Statutory Instrument combining Deusland and Haverfordwest into a new Division to be known as Deusland-Haverfordwest Division.[37] More recently still, in 1986, Mr Douglas Hurd signed a Statutory Instrument amalgamating the former PSDs of Deusland-Haverfordwest, Milford Haven and Pembroke into the new Division of Cleddau, the former PSDs of Fishguard

[35] Scott, op. cit., 7.

[36] SI 1954, no. 1396: Magistrates' Courts: the Petty Sessional Divisions (Pembrokeshire) Order, 1954.

[37] SI 1984, no. 1528: Justices of the Peace, England and Wales: the Petty Sessional Divisions (Dyfed) Order, 1984.

and Cemaes into the new division of Gogledd Preseli, and the former PSDs of Tenby and Narbeth into the new Division of South Pembrokeshire.[38]

So the notion of each of the larger villages having its own bench and courthouse has long disappeared. Indeed, in an age of mass personal transport, such a notion may no longer be valid. Even if the Pembrokeshire magistrates sat in just four locations, Haverfordwest, Tenby, Pembroke and Fishguard, their courts would still be more accessible than many other services, such as hospitals, railway stations, technical colleges, county courts, which are also used on an occasional basis by a minority of the public.[39]

It is also pertinent to point out in this discussion concerning the accessibility of rural courts, that 'much of the business dealt with by the smaller benches could be described as "travelling business" in the sense that the cases had no real local connection'.[40] An analysis of the place of residence of all defendants appearing before the Gogledd Preseli magistrates in 1989 revealed that 56 per cent resided in the area covered by the PSD and 44 per cent outside the area.[41]

Writing in the *Solicitor's Journal* in February 1987, A. N. Pryce warns of the dangers of over-rationalization of courts in rural areas.[42]

> There is little point in the law providing a remedy if it does not provide a realistic opportunity for enforcing that remedy, and this means providing courts where litigants need them, not merely where it may be convenient to provide them.

The accessibility of courthouses is certainly an important issue and it must be considered in any debate concerning the administration of rural justice. Although the closure of courthouses has frequently been a consequence of the amalgamation of PSDs, it need not necessarily be so, and it is a separate issue. The experience of joint domestic and juvenile court panels has shown that it is possible to have one joint panel sitting in a number of locations for the benefit of those using these courts. It is the extension of this principle to the adult criminal courts, namely one relatively large Pembrokeshire bench sitting in a number of different courthouses, that is advocated in this paper. In this way, the interests of defendants, witnesses and

[38] SI, 1986, no. 765: Justices of the Peace, England and Wales: the Petty Sessional Divisions (Dyfed) Order, 1986.

[39] For recent arguments, see *Western Mail*, 13 September 1990.

[40] Scott, op. cit., 23.

[41] Court registers, held in the magistrates' clerk's office in Haverfordwest.

[42] A. N. Pryce, 'Justice in rural areas', *Solicitors' Journal*, 131, 9 (1987), 249–50.

other users of the magistrates' courts can be given due consideration, while at the same time ensuring that the magistrates themselves are not restricted in their experience.

There is just one other aspect of local justice that should perhaps be briefly mentioned, and that is the local knowledge of magistrates. This is not just knowing the pubs, clubs, notorious road junctions, problem estates, wage levels in local industries, but also understanding the local culture and local issues which are of particular significance to the local community. It may be suggested, for example, that a magistrate from Gogledd Preseli would not have the necessary knowledge to sit in Tenby. This must surely be only marginally true and not an insuperable difficulty. Of deeper significance is the need to ensure that the bench as a whole is representative of the local community, in terms of occupation, social class and age. This would be easier to achieve on a larger rather than a smaller bench.

Conclusion

This study has concentrated on the work of a magistrate in a rural area and has suggested ways of overcoming certain disabilities. These suggestions, however, need to be incorporated into a wider policy for rural justice, and such a policy cannot be formulated by a single agency responsible for one part of the court system, such as the magistracy, acting in isolation, on its own. It must involve all justice-related agencies – justices' clerks, the Crown Prosecution Service, police, legal aid and probation services and voluntary agencies working with offenders. 'There is a very great need for the development of appropriate rural justice policies.'[43] It is hoped that this volume will be a starting-point in the formulation of basic principles.

[43] Scott, op. cit., 24.

6

Problems Affecting Rural Policing

PAT HIRST

Introduction

This study is concerned with some of the problems that affect the policing of rural areas, and in particular with those which arise as a result of the constraints imposed by the Police and Criminal Evidence Act 1984 (PACE). The problems encountered by inner-city police forces have been well documented in a number of studies;[1] but rural police forces not only share many of the same problems in implementing the provisions of the 1984 Act, but also have to combat additional difficulties which arise in consequence of their different geographical positions and their relatively restricted manpower levels.

The findings of this study are primarily based on a survey of rural forces in Wales and the south-west of England. Interviews and questionnaires were conducted with a number of officers from these forces, ranging from sergeants to chief constables. It is not in itself a statistical study, but I have been able to draw on the statistics obtained by certain other researchers who have conducted studies of other rural and city forces.

The Police and Criminal Evidence Act

PACE was enacted at the end of October 1984, but the provisions relevant to this study were not brought into force until 1 January 1986.

The Act was passed as an immediate result of the report published

[1] David Brown, *Investigating Burglary: The Effects of PACE*, Home Office Research Study no. 123 (London, 1991).

by the Royal Commission on Criminal Procedure in 1981.[2] It is generally thought that the catalyst for the establishment of this Royal Commission was the notorious *Confait* case (in which innocent teenagers had been convicted of murder on the strength of untrue confessions) and the subsequent Fisher inquiry. Whilst this may have been the immediate catalyst, the pressure for reform of the law governing police powers and criminal procedure had been building up for many years. An earlier Royal Commission had sat in 1960–2 following previous miscarriages of justice which had also drawn attention to the problems of police powers and accountability. On the other hand, police spokesmen, notably Sir Robert Mark, a former Metropolitan Police Commissioner, had protested that the rules of criminal procedure were too heavily weighted in favour of the suspect, and often led to the acquittal of the guilty.

Aims of the Act

PACE accordingly aimed to strike a satisfactory balance between the need to maintain, and in some cases strengthen, police powers to fight crime, and the need to ensure reasonable protection for persons who have been arrested. It was thought that this protection could best be achieved by the imposition of tighter restrictions on the use of the powers of arrest and detention, and by closer regulation of procedures in police stations. PACE and its associated Codes of Practice therefore contain a number of provisions which seek both to strengthen the rights of suspects and to make sure that those rights are respected in practice.

Detention: PACE and the Codes of Practice

Under PACE, persons who have been arrested may be detained for at least as long as is necessary to charge them. Where it is determined that there is sufficient evidence to charge a suspect, he or she should in theory be charged at once, or released (e.g. because the suspect is not going to be charged, or because it has not yet been decided whether charges should be pressed).[3] Where, however, it is considered that there is not yet sufficient evidence to charge the suspect, detention may be prolonged if there are reasonable grounds for believing that this is necessary for the purpose of securing or preserving evidence, or for obtaining evidence by questioning.[4] Such prolongation of the period of detention is subject to strict time limits and, as will be seen, is possible only at certain police stations.

[2] Cmnd 8092.
[3] Police and Criminal Evidence Act 1984, s. 37.
[4] Ibid., s. 38.

The custody officer

Responsibility for ensuring that the provisions of the Act and the Codes of Practice protecting the suspect are observed is placed upon the custody officer. This officer must ordinarily hold at least the rank of sergeant, and when acting as such must ordinarily be uninvolved in the investigation of any crimes of which the persons in his or her custody are suspected or accused.[5]

In addition to determining whether there is sufficient evidence to charge a suspect, or a need to prolong the detention process, the custody officer is responsible for maintaining a 'custody record' for each and every suspect in his or her charge. This record must note everything which happens to the suspect following arrival at the station, and the time at which it happens. It will indicate, for example, whether the suspect has been cautioned and informed of his or her rights, and it will also record more mundane matters such as provision of meals. On top of this, it is the custody officer's responsibility to ensure that order is maintained in the cell block. The custody officer is the key figure in the implementation of the PACE regime.

Designated and non-designated police stations

Until a late stage in its passage through Parliament, the Police and Criminal Evidence Bill made no attempt to distinguish between different types of police station. However, it was eventually recognized that the provision, on a twenty-four-hour basis, of the full range of functions and duties required of a custody officer would impose a wholly intolerable strain on the limited resources of many small rural police stations. Some smaller urban and suburban stations would also be adversely affected. In its final version, the Act therefore distinguishes between 'designated' and 'non-designated' stations.[6]

PACE requires that the chief officer in each area must designate which are to be the stations in that area to be used for the purpose of detaining arrested persons. A sufficient number must be designated to meet the needs of the area, and each designated station must have one or more custody officers.[7] The other, non-designated, stations may still receive prisoners, but only in certain circumstances and only for a maximum period of six hours. One of a number of conditions must be satisfied before an arrested person can lawfully be taken to

[5] Ibid., s. 36.
[6] Ibid., s. 35.
[7] Ibid., s. 30.

a non-designated station.[8] The first is where the arresting officer is working in a locality covered by a non-designated station, unless it appears to him or her that the suspect will have to be held for longer than six hours.[9] The second and third conditions deal with cases in which a single constable, unable to call upon assistance from other officers, considers that an attempt to take the suspect to a designated station would result in the latter injuring himself or herself, the officer or some other person.[10] In all of these cases, the arrested person must eventually be moved to a designated station if it becomes apparent that he or she must be held more than six hours.

At a non-designated station, the duties which would be undertaken by the custody officer at a designated station must be carried out by someone not involved in the investigation of the alleged offence, 'if such an officer is readily available'. If no such officer is available (and in the smallest station this will often be the case) the relevant duties may be carried out by the officer who took the person concerned to the station or by any other officer. Where this occurs, the acting custody officer must, as soon as practicable, notify an officer of the rank of inspector or above at a designated station that this is the case.[11] It will be seen that, at some small stations, every attempt is made to avoid burdening inexperienced officers with the duties of an acting custody officer, and suspects are taken directly to designated stations, even where PACE does not strictly so require.

Problems concerning transportation in rural police areas

As we have already seen, suspects cannot be held for more than six hours at a non-designated station. If the time of detention is going to exceed this limit then the suspect must be transferred to a nearby designated station. In inner city areas this does not cause much of a problem, because the stations are in close proximity to each other. The only problem they may have is to find two officers (driver and escort) for the short time required in order to effect the transfer. In rural areas, however, transfers may involve much greater problems.

To illustrate the problems which rural forces may face in transferring suspects we can look at the Dyfed-Powys police force, which covers a vast rural area of mid- and west Wales. Certain stations in this force may be used as examples. Firstly, let us take the designated station at Aberystwyth and the non-designated station at Lampeter.

[8] Ibid., s. 30(3).
[9] Ibid., s. 30(6).
[10] Ibid., s. 30(5).
[11] Ibid., ss. 30(7), (9), (10).

In geographical terms Aberystwyth station is the nearest designated station to Lampeter at twenty-seven miles away, with the next nearest being thirty miles away at Carmarthen.

Lampeter has the ability to deal with suspects for up to six hours, and has to deal not only with individuals arrested in its own surrounding area, but also with those brought in from the neighbouring areas of Aberaeron and New Quay which are respectively sixteen and twenty miles away. Aberaeron and New Quay have their own non-designated police stations but lack any cell facilities, and are therefore wholly unable to accommodate their own prisoners.

Manpower problems

Many of the problems faced by Aberystwyth and Lampeter are the result of their limited manpower resources. A typical shift at Lampeter station would operate something like this. On the 9 a.m.–5 p.m. and the 5 p.m.–1 a.m. shifts there is usually a full complement on duty consisting of three officers and one sergeant plus any available duty inspector. In addition, there are two traffic officers who patrol the surrounding rural areas. However, it must be remembered that at any given time at least one of these five officers may be unavailable, for any of a number of reasons, including sickness, annual leave, attendance of courses, etc.

From 1 a.m. to 6 a.m. there are usually two officers on duty, but from 6 a.m. to 9 a.m. only one officer will normally be on duty. It is at these times that manpower is at its weakest, but even at times when there is a full shift, the demands of PACE can clearly be significant.

For example, suspects who are to be held for more than six hours must be taken to a designated station at Aberystwyth or Carmarthen. Any suspects who from the moment of arrest seem likely to require detention for a longer period will usually be taken directly to a designated station without being taken to Lampeter first. Others may initially be detained at Lampeter, and transferred only when inquiries are unexpectedly prolonged. In either case, the transfers will ordinarily be carried out by officers from Lampeter. These officers may also be involved in collecting prisoners from New Quay or Aberaeron who are to be held for up to six hours at Lampeter itself.

The consequent strains upon manpower and resources are even greater than one might initially expect. Any such transfer will require a driver and another officer to escort the prisoner. The roads are slow, winding, single carriageways, and a round trip to one of the nearest designated stations may take over two hours.

Furthermore, the police at Lampeter have to transport remand prisoners to the court at Aberaeron. This is not, for once, a PACE-related problem, but stems rather from lack of resources in the prison service. Nevertheless, this may take about one hour, and again at least two officers are required. Indeed, at times the drain upon resources has been such that the only officer available to escort prisoners has been the duty inspector.

The manpower problem is exacerbated at weekends, especially in the summer, when the number of residents in the area is higher and incidents more frequent. This can leave the area seriously underpoliced for a given period of time. When incidents occur at weekends, there is often insufficient manpower available at Lampeter to deal with them, and it becomes necessary for officers from either Carmarthen or Aberystwyth to be called out to assist. This constitutes an inefficient use of scarce resources.

There is yet another complication which may arise from this need to transfer suspects to distant designated stations. Detectives from Lampeter may need to make the same journey at a later stage in order to question the transferred prisoners.

So, would problems be eased by transferring the Lampeter station to designated status? Obviously an immediate advantage would be to eradicate the need to transfer suspects over large distances. But is it practicable or worthwhile to upgrade Lampeter station?

There has been a great deal of discussion within the Dyfed-Powys force about the possible upgrading of Lampeter, but senior officers fear that any such upgrading would probably be supported only by the provision of a single extra uniformed constable. In order to run it properly as a designated station, it would ideally require three or four additional officers, at least one of whom would have to be a sergeant. If those levels of manpower cannot be provided, then the benefits of making Lampeter police station a designated one would be marginal. The advantage of being able to hold prisoners for longer periods would be nullified by the permanent need to tie down experienced sergeants (or at least acting sergeants) in the role of custody officer. PACE does not permit police stations to be operated as designated ones for part of the day (e.g. when a full shift is available) and as non-designated for the rest of the day or night.[12]

A comparison with Aberystwyth is instructive. There are five sergeants at this station, and yet there are times when, owing to sickness, leave, etc., it is unable to provide a sergeant custody

[12] Michael Zander, *The Police and Criminal Evidence Act 1984*, 2nd edn. (London, 1990).

officer throughout the full twenty-four-hour period. At such times, the sergeant at Lampeter may be 'borrowed' in order to cover for the shortage.

Obviously, this is not encouraging in terms of the possibility of upgrading Lampeter. How would the requisite manpower levels be found?

One possible solution might be to provide civilian staff to assist in or take over the transfer of suspects. Such civilians could be employed on lower wages than police officers, but would have to receive some basic training. This proposition is superficially appealing in that the cost of employing a police constable can be in excess of £18,000 per annum, whereas a civilian could be paid less than £10,000. A police constable ought to be free to carry out the police duties for which he is paid and in respect of which the public expect service. The transfer of suspects is not a specialized job and could easily be carried out by a civilian who had received the requisite training. Against this, however, is the fact that such transfers are required only on an irregular basis, and cannot always be carried out at socially acceptable times. Despite the superficial attractions, therefore, it is doubtful whether reliance on civilian drivers and escorts can offer a cost-effective solution to the problem.

The problem of transporting suspects great distances has also been found to trouble the North Wales Police. Once again, round trips of about two hours may be required. A spokesman for North Wales Police asserted that 'round trips of sixty miles or more are sometimes involved and neither the officers nor the vehicle are then available for normal duties to attend to cases for service from the public.' He also went on to say that 'other difficulties occur when detective officers have to travel to designated stations to interview or re-interview prisoners, or when potential witnesses for identification parades have to be transported to such locations.'

Problems of Supervision due to Insufficient Resources

However, these are not the only problems which rural police have to face. The Act also creates difficulties for those designated stations which do not have to transfer suspects. We can take the designated station at Aberystwyth to illustrate the point. Since Aberystwyth station has been chosen as a designated station it is necessary to have a custody officer available at all times in order to receive prisoners. As seen above, Aberystwyth station usually has four to five sergeants as part of its manpower allocation, although at any one time at least one of these will be lost through sickness, annual leave or attendance on courses. Usually there is only one sergeant on each shift. This means that he will generally have to remain in the station to act as custody officer in order to receive suspects.

Police sergeants tend to resent being tied to the station, because, being police officers first and foremost, they will prefer to be out on the beat instead. Since PACE came into force, the Aberystwyth sergeants have had few opportunities to do this. If there is just one prisoner in custody at the station, the duty sergeant will be unable to leave. If there are no such prisoners at the start of his shift, the sergeant can indeed go out; but there may be problems as a result.

Aberystwyth is not a very large town. This is advantageous in some respects, because it means that the sergeant can quickly return to the station if he or she learns that a suspect is being brought in; but at the same time it increases the risk that he or she may become directly involved in an incident leading to one or more arrests. Obviously, this creates difficulties in attempting to comply with the requirements of PACE, which demands that the role of custody officer should be taken on by a police officer who is not involved with the investigation. What happens if the sergeant becomes involved?

The Act allows the duties of custody officer to be performed by any other officer 'if a custody officer is not readily available to perform them', but it is not possible, as at non-designated stations, for one of the arresting officers to perform these duties, and because of the difficulties which inexperienced constables sometimes face in performing this unfamiliar role, the Aberystwyth sergeants try to avoid becoming involved in arrests.

The effective 'chaining' of duty sergeants to the station precincts is unfortunate for reasons other than their own loss of job satisfaction. Obviously, the role of custody officer is central to the operation of PACE, and the sergeant therefore fulfils a very important function in that role. However, a sergeant has always had another important function in the police service, namely as the first line of discipline and management in the service. A sergeant is expected as one of his/her tasks to provide supervision and encouragement to young officers, particularly probationers. Before PACE, the sergeant at Aberystwyth would often be out on patrol in town, thereby providing immediate advice and support to his juniors, and indeed to any special constables on duty at the time. In a place such as Aberystwyth, the sergeant, if out on patrol, could be at the probationer's side in minutes. Now, as a result of the custodial demands of PACE, a constable requiring advice may either radio through to the sergeant at the station or obtain advice from a more experienced fellow constable.

A broadly similar picture emerges at another small non-designated station situated in the Aberystwyth/Carmarthen vicinity, namely that at Cardigan. Cardigan is situated thirty-eight miles from Aberystwyth and thirty miles from Carmarthen. These are, again, the nearest designated stations. There are three sergeants at Cardigan, together with an inspector and five constables; but, as at Aberystwyth, it is unusual for all of the sergeants to be available during any one twenty-four-hour period. With three eight-hour shifts each day, and only two sergeants typically available, it follows that one of these shifts (usually the 1 a.m.–9 a.m. night shift) will not include a sergeant.

Since non-designated stations need not provide a custody officer, it might be thought that the limited availability of sergeants is unimportant. In practice, however, the sergeants tend to remain within the police station for much of the time, particularly when there are prisoners to be taken care of. Drink-driving cases cause further problems. Correct operation of the Lion Intoximeter (the breath analysis machine used to obtain accurate specimens of breath for use as evidence in such cases) is essential if prosecutions are to succeed, and mistakes in the formal procedures accompanying operation of the machine can also result in failure of the prosecution case. Inexperienced operators have been known to ruin the prosecution case, and if a specimen has to be obtained at a time when no sergeant is on duty, the motorist in question will generally be taken all the way to Carmarthen station, in order to be tested.

As at Lampeter, it has been found that considerable time is taken up in transferring prisoners, and detectives from Cardigan also have to travel more in order to carry out interviews of prisoners who have been transferred to a designated station. These are PACE-related problems, but it must be noted that the special problems involving drink-driving cases are not PACE-related at all. The Act has exacerbated certain problems faced by rural police forces, but it would not be fair to blame it for everything. Rural forces are bound to have difficulties in providing a 'full service' for twenty-four hours a day.

Finally, we can look at a rural force area covered by the Devon and Cornwall police. Barnstaple police station and its surrounding area provides the illustration. Barnstaple is the designated station for 'C' Division, and the station covers most of north Devon, including places such as Lynton, Westward Ho, Ilfracombe, Torrington, Bideford and South Molton. All stations other than Barnstaple are non-designated stations. Ilfracombe, for example, is fifteen miles from Barnstaple, and South Molton is nine miles away.

Nearly half of the suspects held at Barnstaple come from Ilfracombe. These are not all suspects who have to be held for more than six hours: as a matter of policy, anyone arrested in the Ilfracombe area between 1 a.m. and 9 a.m. is brought straight to Barnstaple, owing to the fact that the local station has no duty sergeant during those hours. The constables on duty are likely to have little if any experience of the PACE procedures regarding the opening and maintenance of custody records, and despite the time it takes to drive the suspect to Barnstaple (a half-hour round trip), this is considered to be the less inconvenient and less time-consuming option.

Furthermore, between the hours of 9 p.m. and 1 a.m., Ilfracombe will usually only have about three officers on duty. So, if the police arrest an individual and they bring him/her to Barnstaple instead, that will leave only one officer on duty to police a fairly 'rough' area with a population of 10,000. There is some concern over this. It is quite understandably feared that one night an officer could be badly injured through having to attend an incident alone.

Published Research Findings upon the Effects of PACE in relation to the Transportation of Suspects

As we have seen, suspects have to be transported between stations in the same force area for a number of reasons, and this constitutes a demand on police resources. A significant portion of this demand may arise from the requirements of PACE. David Brown, in a study of English forces carried out for the Home Office, found that on average 3 per cent of suspects in his survey had been held elsewhere in the same force.[13] In some cases, the figure was higher, but not greater than 7 per cent for any one force. According to Brown's research, it was not always easy to work out from the custody records whether the reason for the transfer was that the six-hour limit on detention at a non-designated station had been exceeded. He nevertheless concludes that it is safe to assume that this was not the reason behind the transfers of those who had been held elsewhere for more than six hours.

Some two-thirds of the transfers in Brown's survey were of suspects who had been detained elsewhere for a shorter period, and were therefore possible PACE-related transfers: just 2 per cent of the total number of suspects held.

These figures do not appear to suggest the existence of a major

[13] Brown, *Investigating Burglary*.

problem, but they are of course average figures which reflect the large number of arrests in major urban forces. Brown's study showed that in Hampshire and Cambridgeshire, for example, two sub-divisional designated stations which covered quite large rural areas accounted for most of the transfers to sampled stations in these forces. The figures show that 33 per cent and 11 per cent respectively were of suspects who had previously been held at undesignated stations.

Furthermore, in one respect at least, the figures produced by Brown may be misleading, because it has been demonstrated that many of the suspects arrested within the areas covered by non-designated stations are never held at those stations. If it is clear that they will need to be held for a lengthy period, or if, as at Ilfracombe, the policy is not to burden inexperienced officers with the complexities of the PACE custody procedure, persons arrested in the areas covered by non-designated stations will be taken directly to the nearest designated station, and the custody record opened there will not show a 'transfer' at all.

Some research on this area has been carried out by police officers themselves. Sergeant Peter MacKay of Bedfordshire police studied procedures in his own force area.[14] He found that, whereas the force as a whole was not greatly burdened by the need to transfer suspects from non-designated stations to designated ones, some non-designated stations had to transfer up to one-third of their suspects. This finding is consistent with the estimates provided by officers in Dyfed-Powys and north Devon.

Possible Solutions

Because of their smaller populations and frequently lower crime rates, it is inevitable that manpower resources in rural police areas will be relatively low. PACE cannot be blamed for this. It can be said, however, that certain requirements of the Act place a proportionately greater strain on the thinly spread resources of the rural police.

It is clear that the initial versions of the Police Bill failed to take account of the different position of the rural forces. The concept of the non-designated station, introduced at a late stage in its passage through Parliament, was intended to represent a concession to the problems faced by smaller police stations (both rural and urban) which could not be expected to provide custody officers and associated facilities for suspects on a twenty-four-hour basis.

[14] Study by Peter McKay for Bedfordshire Police.

But, whereas a small urban station might be expected to have a larger designated station a short distance away from it, and would therefore benefit very clearly from the concession, the remote rural station tends to lose out either way: if designated, it needs increased manpower, or will at least find that its duty sergeants spend almost all their time on custody officer duties; if not designated, it will lose some of its already thin manpower every time a suspect has to be taken on a lengthy drive to the nearest designated station.

The use of civilian drivers and/or escorts might sometimes be a partial solution; but, as previously explained, the irregular nature of the work seems to preclude this as a general solution. The use of civilians as custody officers is another matter. There could be obvious financial savings (relative to the salaries of a sergeant), and more stations could perhaps be designated as a result, but even those sergeants who most regret being tied to custody duties flinch from the idea. It would require significant amendment to PACE and a departure from historic practice. Some alternative amendments to PACE might provide less drastic solutions. Lengthening the permitted period of detention at non-designated stations to, say, eight hours would be of very limited help, since few transfers would be avoided in that way. A more promising possible amendment could be one which enabled stations to be designated for periods of each day, and to operate as non-designated stations at other times (e.g. during the early hours of the morning, when available manpower is usually at its lowest).

It would be wrong to suggest that the rural police forces face a major crisis as a result of the existing rules. What perhaps can be said is that the rural forces now operate in a legal regime designed to govern the quite different problems of the inner cities, and it is not one which suits them.

7

Non-statutory Support for Victims and Offenders

LYNNE HURLEY

One of the most interesting developments in recent years in the criminal justice system has been the changing balance between statutory and non-statutory provision. This study deals with one aspect of this development, the parallel growth and decline of two notable non-statutory agencies as observed within two Welsh districts. In the geographical areas within which this study is set, the districts of Ceredigion and Montgomery in mid-Wales, assistance for victims of crime is provided by a number of organizations, all non-statutory. Valuable work is done by the three Welsh Women's Aid groups in the area, and by the Rape Crisis Line in Aberystwyth. It is not the intention of this study, however, to describe the work of these agencies, which are outside the mainstream of the criminal justice system and which may themselves have an ideological objection to the use of the term 'victim'. Consequently attention will be concentrated upon Victim Support, which has schemes in each of the areas in question.

By contrast, non-statutory provision for offenders is presently meagre and soon to become non-existent. In the absence of Apex Trust (the agency which offers work experience for offenders) and of any similar body, the only organization which has operated in the area in recent years is the National Association for the Care and Resettlement of Offenders (NACRO). It is proposed, therefore to examine the functions of NACRO and Victim Support and to compare their respective development. There is, of course, a statutory agency entrusted with the care of offenders, the Probation Service, but it is insufficiently resourced to become involved in many of the activities in which NACRO engages. The apparent polarization of NACRO and the National Association of Victim Support Schemes (NAVSS) would appear at first sight to make them unlikely candidates for comparison, but in terms of their status as voluntary bodies they are much closer in orientation than might be expected. Moreover, they share a history which perhaps accounts for the many similarities of structure and of style which characterize their national organizations.

Hatch's attempt (1980) to distinguish between the different types of voluntary organizations in existence within the British welfare system was further developed by Brenton (1985), who advanced the proposition that the 'ideal type' of voluntary body should have come into existence independently of the state, and be constitutionally separate from government, self-governing, non-profit-distributing and of public benefit. Gill and Mawby (1990) have considered the complexities of such categorization and have devised a typology which places NACRO and Victim Support in close proximity in two out of four dimensions. With regard to the source of funding, on a continuum from 'self-supporting' to 'state funding', they are both located towards the latter end; and when considering the relationship between helper and helped, the two are located together in a central position on a continuum from 'fellowship' to 'professional–client'. When examining the goals of voluntary agencies, Gill and Mawby locate NACRO and Victim Support centrally on a continuum from 'social movement' to 'social provision' but in this instance they are somewhat further apart, with NACRO nearer the former and Victim Support nearer the latter.

In so far as NACRO and Victim Support are able to be classified in this way, they can be said to share many common elements in their status as voluntary organizations. Furthermore, as Victim Support travels down the well-worn path of increasing dependence upon central government funding, attention should perhaps be drawn to the experiences of local NACRO schemes and their dependence upon the state for subsistence.

Rock (1990) charts the origins of the NAVSS and acknowledges that the internal structure of the organization was largely formulated by NACRO employees, seconded for a time to oversee the development of this new body. In time both agencies came to enjoy the benefits of having a close relationship with the Home Office and also to suffer the consequences. In Rock's view:

> Although they have not silenced themselves, the staff of NACRO do understand that they must be circumspect. They cannot be too loudly political or critical in their utterances about criminal justice policy.

> NACRO is not so much a pressure group as a supplier, tester, critic, and creator of services. (p. 138)

NACRO's commitment to 'sobriety and restraint' was bequeathed to the NAVSS and was assiduously maintained, partly in order to avoid engendering an unnecessary fear of crime but also in recognition that 'officials and politicians attached to the Home Office evince a marked propensity to flinch in the face of stridency' (Rock 1990, p. 226). The two organizations have differed, however, in the amount of bureaucratic control that each has managed to exert over its composite schemes. The NAVSS has maintained its original brief as an advisory body to promote a competent, standardized system of provision and to disseminate information for and about victims. Even with a carrot to dangle before local groups, the responsibility for allocation of government grants, it has never been in a position to direct its volunteer 'workforce' in the way that NACRO is able closely to monitor its paid employees.

The Origins of Victim Support

Victim Support in Britain can be traced back to 1969 when a victim–offender study group was formed in Bristol by regional officers of the South Wales and Severn Region of the National Association for the Care and Resettlement of Offenders. This study group was partly motivated by criticisms of penal groups for their apparent lack of concern for the needs of victims (Holtom and Raynor 1988), and concerned that a deficiency of recognition and representation may in some way contribute to a hardening of attitudes towards offenders. Discovery of the extent of the neglect suffered by victims confirmed the group in its belief that a void needed to be filled.

A schism developed almost immediately (Rock 1990), resulting in two attempts to instigate pilot projects and two attempts to form national organizations. An advice centre in Kingswood, Gloucestershire was opened in November 1973, and the National Victims' Association was established, but both were short-lived. Bristol Association for the Care and Resettlement of Offenders, meanwhile, had maintained its interest in the concept of victim support, and while no immediate steps had been taken to follow through the ideas of the victim–offender group, the impact of these preliminary studies led to the South West Council of NACRO setting up a working party to instigate a pilot project for the care of victims of crime. Bristol Victim Support Scheme (BVSS) eventually came into existence in December 1973 and began operating in the next year.

Certain principles were adopted immediately. Its management committee was to reflect a cross-section of informed opinion, drawing heavily on probation and police expertise. Support for victims would be mainly short-term, so as to encourage them to draw away from the victim role. Long-term support, except in special cases, would reinforce the stereotype. The policy of 'outreach' was devised, which meant that the onus was upon volunteers to make contact with victims and not vice versa. Victims of vehicle-related crime were excluded from having home visits because there was little evidence of their need for support, and because the success of BVSS in attracting victims had resulted in a policy of prioritizing certain categories of victims whose needs were deemed to be greatest. Liaison with Bristol South-West police division yielded a small but regular supply of victims' names every week.

In 1979, five years after Bristol, the National Association of Victim Support Schemes was brought into existence with the active encouragement of NACRO (Rock 1990), which had always recognized the need to distance itself from victim support. Creation of a national organization for the BVSS and the thirty or so other groups which had sprung up in its wake was seen as a positive means of achieving complete autonomy for victim support. The NAVSS consciously aimed to further the 'needs' of victims, unlike victim movements in the United States and Canada where there is much more forceful emphasis upon 'rights' and a greater inclination to become involved in wider aspects of the criminal justice system (Normandeau 1989). Resistance to involvement in these issues in Britain was to prove a source of strength for the NAVSS. Growth during the 1980s was remarkable: in 1984 there were about 200 affiliated schemes (NAVSS undated), and by the end of 1990 there were 363 operating in England, Wales and Northern Ireland (NAVSS 1990)

BVSS was to be the model for most of those which followed. Its problems more often than not became theirs: dependence upon the police for a supply of victims' names could mean establishing contact only with those who had previously been 'filtered' by local officers – the 'less deserving', and those considered to have suffered from crimes too serious to be within the remit of victim support being excluded; too close an affinity with the 'ideal victim' – elderly, vulnerable, blameless, at the expense of less obvious but equally deserving victims, was to leave the movement open to criticism; and constant fund-raising, essential even for an organization with a relatively 'safe' cause, was a time-consuming activity.

These problems and others were inherited by the many schemes which followed. In some cases, they were never overcome. But the strengths of Bristol were also inherited. Victim Support encompassed what is essentially a single-issue cause and filled a very real gap in welfare provision. Schemes are affiliated to the NAVSS if they fulfil certain criteria, including the provision of training for volunteers and the establishment of a management committee. Day-to-day operational decisions are in the hands of the scheme co-ordinators, work which often had to be done in the past by a volunteer but which has been an established post since the granting of Home Office funding in 1987.

NAVSS increasingly identifies and prioritizes issues for debate, which were previously targeted by individual schemes on an *ad hoc* basis, in an attempt to promote a uniformity of provision for victims. More assistance is being offered to non-crime victims, particularly victims of road traffic accidents, and the national organization is hoping to draw upon the expertise of pressure groups such as the Campaign Against Drinking and Driving. The organization is entering into discussions with the police, social services, Women's Aid and others, with a view to encouraging its schemes to become more involved with victims of domestic violence. Moving into this arena presents volunteers with a number of difficulties, however, not the least of which is the problem of access to the victim, given that the usual mode of response is for a home visit. The suitability of operational techniques such as 'crisis intervention' is called into question, but the attractiveness of providing a variety of options for victims of domestic violence may overwhelm local opposition. Past research has favoured 'choice' for other types of victim, such as those who are suffering from the effects of rape (Maguire and Corbett 1987).

The History and Development of NACRO

NACRO was formally constituted in March 1966, during a special general meeting of the National Association of Discharged Prisoners Aid Societies, which had been called in order to dissolve itself. This was the co-ordinating body for the voluntarily run Prisoners Aid Societies and it had become virtually redundant following implementation of an ACTO (Advisory Council on the Treatment of Offenders) Report.[1] The primary aims of the new organization were to foster closer co-operation between the voluntary and

[1] The Discharged Prisoners' Aid Societies had been criticized before the publication of *The Organisation of After-Care*, the report of the Home Office Advisory Council on the Treatment of Offenders (London, 1963). By 1966 the probation and after-care service had taken on many of the functions of the DPAs, leaving them increasingly marginalized.

statutory sectors and to act as an umbrella body to co-ordinate voluntary effort in the field of after-care of prisoners (NACRO 1967).

For the first six years of its existence, much of NACRO's work echoed the traditional concerns of penal reform groups: the state of prisons; the prison building programme; and the welfare of prisoners and ex-prisoners. It remained essentially an umbrella group; it initiated projects but ran none of its own. Then, in 1972, a significant policy decision was taken by NACRO which involved both an overhaul of its bureaucracy and the establishment of its own projects. The first of these was LANCE, a housing initiative for the single homeless in Manchester, the earliest of a number of hostels designed as an attempt to overcome accommodation difficulties faced by offenders and those considered to be 'at risk'.

Government funding allowed NACRO to expand its commitment to education both inside prison and in the community. Education centres were established under the auspices of the Voluntary Projects Programme (VPP), including three in Wales, at Newport, Pontypridd and Swansea. Tuition was provided by volunteers, often unemployed themselves, and by NACRO staff. Activities were rarely confined to literacy and numeracy; an early report from a NACRO education project claimed to provide cookery, art, music, drama and sports (NACRO 1981), and VPP centres continued in this tradition, adding, among other subjects, computing, video and photography, motor mechanics and black studies to the curriculum (NACRO 1986). When VPP folded, along with the Community Programme, NACRO continued its commitment to education with its National Education Advisory Service (funded by the Home Office) and a small number of education projects (none in Wales), firmly believing that 'education has an important part to play in the resettlement of offenders – by developing skills, confidence and interests and by concentrating on their capacity, potential and future rather than on their past, problems and weaknesses' (NACRO 1988, 10).

NACRO enjoys a higher media profile for its crime prevention and related work. It has had a Safe Neighbourhood Unit to liaise with local authorities on the implementation of crime prevention strategies and currently has twelve Youth Activities Units for the development of initiatives for children and young people on disadvantaged estates (NACRO 1990). A Welsh Juvenile Crime Section operates in south Wales, funded by the Welsh Office.

The publication by NACRO of *Diversion from Criminal Justice in an English Context* (Zander 1975), examined ways of translating into a British context United States experiences of a decade or more of 'New Careers' activity. New Careers, originally designed as an anti-poverty programme (Pearl and Reissman 1965), had inspired a pioneer project in a California prison to formulate a programme for training offenders during incarceration and after release, with the eventual aim of these offenders becoming aides to professionals working in welfare agencies (Hodgkin 1971). By this stage, NACRO had already initiated two diversion projects which had gone some way to promote New Careers, the Bristol New Careers Project, started in 1973, and the Hammersmith Teenage Project, established at the end of 1974.

It is likely, however, that more general provision for the employment and training of offenders would have remained patchy but for the creation of the Manpower Services Commission (MSC) in 1973. The MSC was intended to be the co-ordinating body for industrial sector training but in fact became the instigator of temporary work experience and training courses, with special emphasis on youth training (Finegold and Soskice 1988). Its budget rose from £125 million in 1974–5 to £641 million in 1978–9. NACRO was endowed with the resources to expand its services, by involvement in a series of MSC employment measures, including the Job Creation Programme, the Special Temporary Employment Programme, the Community Programme and, currently, Employment Training. Expansion was striking, particularly under the Community Programme, transforming NACRO into a much more complex organization. Its considerable financial responsibilities set it apart from other agencies in the criminal justice system (Ryan 1983).

The MSC announced the introduction of the Community Programme in July 1982, and within four months NACRO had agreed to become a national agency for the management of the new programme. A Community Programme Section was established by the end of 1982, and by the end of March 1983 twenty-five schemes were being sponsored, providing 2,600 places 'primarily to provide employment opportunities for long-term unemployed offenders and to provide services and facilities for disadvantaged areas' (NACRO 1983, 8). The schemes were to carry out work within certain designated categories which included environmental improvements, energy conservation and insulation, recycling of waste materials and crime prevention schemes. A consequence of Community Programme (CP) funding was the virtual coverage by NACRO schemes of the whole of England and Wales.

NACRO's strong emphasis on access to education facilities continued for both CP and Youth Training Scheme (YTS) participants, with a particular recognition of the educational shortcomings of the average offender. Ideas about the teaching of literacy and numeracy and concepts such as 'personal effectiveness' moved across from VPP and permeated the CP. On average, participants in NACRO'S CP schemes had fewer qualifications than participants in schemes sponsored by other agencies. In January 1988, NACRO provided for 20,000 people on CP and YTS, and of these 60 per cent had no educational qualifications whatsoever, and 80 per cent had no vocational qualifications. Over half of these people were recent known offenders (NACRO 1989).

The CP ended in September 1988 and, unlike NACRO, many other CP managers had inadequate resources to move into Employment Training. For those who were able, greater restrictions on funding exacerbated the strains of attempting to sell a scheme which aroused controversy before it started (*Guardian*, 15 April 1988). Employment Training was unpopular with the unemployed, and four months after it began, a campaign was under way to increase trainee numbers (*Times*, 30 December 1988). But attracting trainees was to remain an uphill struggle, and this, together with the rigour of the schemes, had far-reaching effects on NACRO's Employment Training centres. Mid-Wales was to be among the first areas to experience the effects of diminishing resources.

Local Provision: Victim Support

North Powys Victim Support Scheme, whose boundaries more or less coincide with the borders of Montgomery, was set up in 1985 and is based in Newtown. It is one of four schemes which cover the whole of Powys, the others being at Brecon, Ystradgynlais and Llandrindod Wells. Dyfed Victim Support Scheme, to include Ceredigion, began operation in May 1991.

North Powys was run entirely by voluntary effort until a government grant in June 1988 enabled it to appoint a full-time co-ordinator. As this grant covered only the co-ordinator's expenses, constant fund-raising remained essential to cover volunteers' expenses and the scheme's bills. Nowadays this is normally achieved by regular approaches to town and community councils and by one big fund-raising event a year, in conjunction with the three other Powys schemes. Rent-free premises are provided by Montgomery District Council. From interviews conducted with the co-ordinator and on examination of data provided, North Powys gives the appearance of being an efficient, successful scheme. In national terms, it has a good flow of work for a rural area, dealing with 1,012 referrals in 1990, the highest figure of all four Powys schemes. This figure includes a small proportion of non-crime victims, usually casualties or witnesses of road traffic accidents. For these victims, emotional support may be supplemented with practical help. There are regular requests for assistance at inquests, either to escort a victim or relative, or to explain procedures.

A further forty-seven other victims were passed for assistance to other areas. The scheme also accepts self-referrals, and while it does not go out of its way to encourage them, it is regularly contacted for this purpose by agencies such as the Citizens' Advice Bureaux. This allows the scheme to tackle the issue of unreported crime, albeit in a very minor way. Long-term assistance is maintained only in exceptional circumstances. Normal practice is for one or two visits per victim. In the first quarter of 1991, referral figures were up by 10 per cent. The co-ordinator is satisfied with the workload, but he has an increasingly heavy commitment of meetings, courses and conferences, which prevents him from having much direct contact with victims, as was originally the case.

In common with many other rural areas, north Powys has a plentiful supply of volunteers, with a minimal turnover. There is a nucleus of twelve; five of these, including the co-ordinator, are completely trained in all aspects of victim support, and this includes more skilled techniques such as rape counselling; the remaining seven are at various stages in the process of becoming fully trained. Around this nucleus is a more than adequate number of other volunteers, often recruited by the co-ordinator from participants at the many meetings he attends. 'Homewatch' meetings are particularly lucrative in terms of interest. There are no known ex-victims amongst the volunteers, either past or present. They have never been discounted, and their future presence is not ruled out; their absence may have some correlation with the study of victim support in the south-west of England by Mawby and Gill (1987), which found little evidence that volunteers are motivated to work with schemes because of previous victimization.

Induction for all volunteers is based, in the first instance, on the NAVSS Training Manual and is delivered by the co-ordinator. Training is not restricted to the manual, however, as outsiders with a relevant input are recruited to provide courses, and these range from the police and probation to Rape Crisis Centres. Subsequent training given to volunteers is based on an assessment of their natural skills and on their level of commitment. The co-ordinator holds regular meetings with small groups of volunteers in each part of this large rural area on a monthly basis, or more frequently if required. The volunteers have a representative on the local management committee.

The national association, unlike its counterpart in NACRO,

continues to exert limited control over its affiliated groups. The allocation of government funding enables it to demand certain standards of procedure but its role remains an advisory one and it provides no directed training and, at least in the experience of north Powys, exercises no quality control. Without this mechanism, quality of provision is largely at the discretion of individual schemes.

A profile of the volunteers reveals a reasonable cross-section of the local population. In the past some Victim Support schemes have been heavily dependent upon the elderly, retired volunteer (Mawby and Gill 1987), understandably given their availability. In rural areas a noticeable proportion of this group are likely to be in-migrants; in rural Wales sensible public relations dictates that the indigenous population should be a visible part of any organization which is seeking popular support. The scheme, consciously or unconsciously, avoids this possible source of conflict. Volunteers include locals and incomers; working people, both professional and manual workers; the retired; and mothers of schoolchildren. Welsh-speakers are in the minority but are available, particularly in and around places like Machynlleth, where they are more likely to be in demand. There is a large proportion of women volunteers, perhaps inevitably, although this may also be as a result of the deliberate policy of the scheme which seeks to match a woman victim with a woman volunteer for all crimes and not just those of a sexual nature.

Academic debate surrounding victim support has concentrated upon referral systems and selectivity of victim at scheme level. In the past the more organized schemes were encouraged by the NAVSS to press their local police forces for ‘automatic’ or ‘blanket’ referral (Maguire and Corbett 1987), which meant that all victims of certain, agreed categories of crime would have their names passed to victim support. ‘Selective’ referral, meaning either the acquisition of victims’ names only with their prior consent, or the filtering of victim information by the police themselves, was less satisfactory.

Over three-quarters of the schemes now have a policy of automatic referral ageed with their local police forces, partly, perhaps, because the employment of paid co-ordinators promotes a more ‘professional’ image, but variations in police attitude to victim support still exists. The North Wales Police Force refers very few victims to Gwynedd Victim Support, despite the fact that it is now a well-established scheme. By contrast, schemes such as north Powys enjoy a far better relationship with the local force. Referral from Dyfed-Powys Police Force is automatic in both policy and practice. There are only two categories of victim excluded at present: those who have suffered domestic violence, and victims of child abuse. Even here the situation is far from clear-cut. The police are attempting to move away from their policy of referring all victims of domestic violence to the local Women's Aid Group, towards a multi-agency approach. This is a development the north Powys co-ordinator does not particularly welcome, as an appropriate response to this type of victim is more time-consuming than is normal for traditional short-term victim support. But despite some misgivings, talks concerning this issue are under way in many areas. In cases of alleged child abuse, the police contact the social services, but it has been known for North Powys Victim Support to become involved at a later stage.

Every weekday morning the co-ordinator attends the police station in order to collect particulars of all crime committed since the previous visit. The scheme receives a copy of the crime report sheet. The police send details about victim support to all victims, but as the policy of north Powys is to make immediate contact, it is common for people to be visited before they are in receipt of the police leaflet. The scheme does try to make initial contact by phone, but if this is impossible victims are approached without prior warning. In its experience, this procedure works successfully and is not considered by victims to be intrusive.

The scheme contacts all referrals either by post or in person, and three times a week the co-ordinator meets with the volunteer who has the job of ensuring that contact is established. The types of crime victims encountered by the scheme more or less conform to the national picture of victim support referrals (NAVSS 1990). Crimes involving theft of/from vehicles and damage to them were estimated to account for one-third of all crimes examined in the last *British Crime Survey* (1988). Victims of vehicle crime have always been too numerous to deal with in person, and few of these have ever required help, but a letter is sent by north Powys, thereby placing the onus upon the victim to make further contact should support be needed.

Victims of burglary, particularly the residential kind, have always accounted for the greater part of the workload of victim support, an occurrence welcomed by some schemes as burglary is a crime which is serious enough for volunteers to get their teeth into without requiring a high degree of skill (Maguire and Corbett 1987). A consequence of automatic referral has been to make past criticisms of an overemphasis on burglary victims less of an issue. Victims of burglary remain the largest percentage of referrals for north Powys but the scheme deals increasingly with victims of assaults and of criminal damage.

More controversial has been the issue of selection of victim, both by the scheme and by the police. Christie (1986) defines the 'ideal victim' as being weak – old, sick or very young – carrying out a respectable project in a location where he or she could not possibly be blamed for being. Being attacked by an unknown offender fits the 'ideal' because it leaves little room for complicity. The plight of the elderly victim, with or without the rest of these attributes, was seized upon by many early schemes, encouraged by police attitudes. This continued despite growing evidence that they suffer fewer crimes (with the exception of personal theft) than younger people (Maxfield 1984), even when they place themselves in potentially vulnerable situations (Clarke *et al.* 1985). A recognition that fear of crime may make the elderly indirect victims of crime does not detract from the argument that victim support concentrates resources upon the elderly at the expense of less appealing victims. Young males compose the most victimized group and, paradoxically, the most likely group to be the perpetrators of crime (Fattah 1989).

Shifting the onus of responsibility from police to scheme by means of automatic referral does not necessarily result in moral objectivity on this issue, but the north Powys scheme demonstrates an awareness of the problem and a willingness to try to tackle it. The scheme selects its clients only on the basis of seriousness of crime; victims of vehicle crime do not automatically receive a visit, but most other victims do. This policy decision removes the burden of selection from the co-ordinator and secures a service for sections of the population which are less obviously in need of assistance. Volunteers have visited young male victims who, in previous cases in which the scheme has been involved, have been the offenders. Accepting self-referrals is one way of tackling the problem of under-reporting by these victims.

Victim dissatisfaction with the role of the police is well charted (Maguire 1982; Shapland *et al.* 1985; Newburn and Merry 1990). Prosecution of an offender can be considered less important than the manner in which a case is handled. Particular attention has been paid to the lack of information for victims in two respects: notification by the police of the apprehension or charging of a suspect or, conversely, a decision to terminate inquiries; and, information about the date and time of the trial and the outcome of the case. It has been found that victims consider dialogue on these central issues to be of relevance in the process of recovery. Dyfed-Powys police has no system, at the present time, to ensure that victims are updated and North Powys Victim Support keeps them informed only if specifically requested to do so by an individual victim, but the Powys schemes are shortly to meet with the Crown Prosecution

Service for discussions on the 'Victim's Charter'[2] and these issues will be under review.

Local Provision: NACRO

The NACRO schemes in mid-Wales all had their origins in the Community Programme. NACRO Aberystwyth worked in Ceredigion and in part of Meirionnydd. NACRO Powys operated in the Montgomery and Radnor areas of Powys. Wales was separated into two regions, north and south, until the end of 1988, and Aberystwyth and Powys were part of the south Wales region. In terms of numbers, these schemes were never more than small-to-medium providers, but the geographical area they covered was extensive. All three schemes engaged in work which was, according to MSC definitions, of benefit either to the local community or to individuals in receipt of designated state benefits. Restoration work in churchyards, improvements to village halls and draughtproofing the homes of those on supplementary benefit were activities common to all three. Other tasks might include painting, decorating and gardening. The amount of skills involved varied from project to project, and the transference of those skills was dependent upon the quality of supervision.

With regard to division of labour along gender lines, these schemes differed little from other NACRO schemes (Crow *et al.* 1989). NACRO first adopted its Equal Opportunities Statement in 1983 but, despite this, men composed the majority on the types of project which involved manual work. Females tended to be concentrated in office administration projects and in the provision of welfare facilities.

Anyone over eighteen years of age was eligible for the CP assuming that he/she had been unemployed for six months if under twenty-five, or for twelve months if aged over twenty-five. As the MSC insisted upon an average wage of £67 per week, most jobs were part-time, inevitably making the CP more attractive to the young and unmarried.

More specialist and certified training in subjects such as supervisory skills and first aid was made available by NACRO, but the acquisition of a formal training qualification was not considered a necessity by the MSC. Unlike YTS, the CP was very much a 'work experience' scheme, and NACRO, with its high proportion of the 'disadvantaged', both offender and non-offender, promoted the teaching of 'basic' or

[2] The 'Victim's Charter', published by the Home Office in 1990, outlines recommendations for good practice and interprets the role of Victim Support schemes.

'life' skills, which might include instruction on welfare benefits, as well as awareness on the social problems of drug and alcohol abuse and AIDS.

All NACRO initiatives, including the CP, are open to the non-offender. Early in its development, the organization adhered to the theory of 'labelling', believing that maintaining offender-only projects might reinforce the stereotype and that people felt to be 'at risk' of offending should also be considered for assistance. Despite any shortcomings that labelling theory may have (Box 1987) NACRO's employment schemes have continued to encourage a 'quota' of offenders to work or train alongside other long-term unemployed people. During the course of CP the Welsh schemes tended to attract a high proportion, which had some bearing on how scheme managers focused on their needs (Crow *et al.* 1989). Offenders are believed to have played a more central role in Wales, whereas in regions where the proportion was lower, they are more likely to have been regarded as part of a wider, disadvantaged group.

There was, however, considerable variation from scheme to scheme within the south Wales region as to the proportion of offenders employed. During the last eight months of the programme, the schemes had an average proportion of offenders as follows:[3]

Aberystwyth	34.9%	Mid Glamorgan	34.3%
Barry	40%	Milford Haven	28.6%
Cardiff	39.6%	Powys	26.3%
Gwent	68%	West Glamorgan	32.7%

While the proportion of offenders in Powys was probably typical of a rural area, Aberystwyth (which included a base at Lampeter but not Cardigan), had a surprisingly high proportion. During this period it was on a par with Mid Glamorgan, which included Merthyr Tydfil, and it exceeded the offender/non-offender ratio in West Glamorgan, which took in Swansea. This was not, of course, a typical period, as one employment programme was running down in order to be replaced by another, but although the proportion of offenders may have been, at times, somewhat higher in Mid and West Glamorgan, in Aberystwyth a figure of 34.9 per cent would not have been considered unusual throughout the CP.

The CP was never intended to provide skills training. It supplied work experience for up to a year, with pay negotiated at the local

[3] These percentages are based on monthly returns made by the schemes to the Welsh regional office from January to August 1988.

'rate for the job'. Participants were aware of its limitations: few jobs were extended for more than a year but for non-offenders it offered a more interesting alternative to being on the dole; and for offenders it presented a way of paying off fines, or even a means of avoiding a custodial sentence. Although research indicates that the CP was being used by the probation service and its clients more as a form of post-sentence provision, some NACRO CP schemes came to be regarded by the courts as part of a viable non-custodial alternative (Crow *et al.* 1989).

Earlier research by Soothill and Holmes (1981) suggested that if the rate of recidivism is to be reduced, then offenders must secure good-quality employment rather than low-skilled, menial jobs. But pragmatism demands that the best has to be made of what is on offer. In rural areas such as mid-Wales, what was on offer during the mid 1980s was the CP and very little else. Unemployment is a universal blight, but it is a particular problem for offenders. Recent findings from NACRO indicate that known offenders coming to the organization for training have, on average, fewer qualifications than non-offenders, have less stable work patterns and endure greater lengths of unemployment.[4] For many low achievers, a supportive environment can be particularly helpful until a normal work pattern is established or re-established, and the programme was intended to sustain participants in this way. For NACRO, the CP offered an opportunity to present offenders in a more flattering perspective: working in their local communities improving the environment; refurbishing socially useful facilities like community centres and church halls; and helping to ameliorate inadequate conditions in the homes of the aged and deprived.

Allowing offenders to have such close links with their communities was potentially problematic. A balance had to be found between maintaining confidentiality about known offenders, with supervision when they were working in local homes. It is notable that Crow *et al.* (1989) found that over three-quarters of known offenders, as opposed to about a half of non-offenders, were allocated to NACRO's manual projects. These largely consisted of outdoor work. NACRO had a policy as to which members of staff should be informed of the presence on the scheme of a known offender; in practice it was very much at the discretion of the manager and, at least in the rural Wales schemes, it was commonplace during the CP for each supervisor and leading-hand to know exactly which members of his or her team were ex-offenders. Moreover, there was

[4] Information taken from NACRO's internal monitoring reports, 'New careers employment training programme, analysis of trainee records', for the period September 1988 to September 1989.

usually little opportunity of preventing the vast majority of staff and participants knowing the same, given the nature of rural life. When NACRO moved into Employment Training the situation worsened. Trainees were to be found training places with private employers, and if a lack of mobility militated against travelling long distances, then local businesses were the only option. Finding a training place for an offender in the more rural areas could be extremely difficult when the local community knew not merely the identity of offenders but the exact nature of their convictions. Unless an atmosphere of greater tolerance prevails, 'confidentiality' is likely to remain an irresolvable problem in rural areas.

The CP had the explicit aim of engendering good working habits in the long-term unemployed. Throughout the programme, participants were actively encouraged to consider their futures. Managing agents, NACRO included, taught techniques such as 'interviewing skills' and produced 'job search' training packages. Although further education was encouraged as one option at the end of the programme, the most sought-after outcome was to secure full-time, permanent employment.

The study by Crow *et al.* (1989) was an analysis of NACRO's YTS and CP schemes and it found that a quarter of all leavers from NACRO CP schemes went directly into a job or further training and that in Wales, an unusually high proportion secured employment, both offenders and non-offenders. This was not necessarily the case in rural mid-Wales. Here it was usual to see participants leave CP and return when re-eligible. If non-offenders were finding it too difficult to gain employment, then it is not unreasonable to surmise that people with an offending background, and with the additional burdens of poor qualifications and a less than glowing job history, would find life even tougher. In rural Wales, the CP was a means of subsisting, and it is doubtful that anyone, staff or participant, was under any other illusion.

Crow *et al.* found that NACRO employment schemes had only a very limited success in reducing the rate of recidivism, and concede that it is perhaps too much to expect schemes of this duration to have a desirable outcome in terms of recidivism, believing that we should see them as an integral part of a more general provision for offenders. A more cynical view is that it is probably better to have offenders engaged in some form of meaningful activity than out on the streets. It would, however, have been worthwhile if the CP had helped in some way to improve the economic position of offenders by enabling them to acquire more marketable skills. Instead, these types of programmes provided work experience which did little to help the disadvantaged to get a foot on the ladder of social stability.

They remained on the margins, engaging in peripheral economic activity, in a secondary market for the unskilled and those with outdated skills. Consequently,

> Sponsoring work within this secondary market may therefore be seen as assisting in a process of supportive adjustment to the pressure of economic decline and restructuring, rather than a pushing forward new avenues of economic development or challenging the forces giving rise to economic stresses and strains. (Crow *et al.* 1989, 137)

Put another way, NACRO staff in areas such as rural Wales were trying to help many participants on the schemes adjust to a life on the dole, and they probably realized as much.

A problem common to all voluntary agencies in mid-Wales is that operating in a large rural area with scattered communities makes personal communication an expensive business. Travelling expenses are a constant drain on resources, and parent organizations tend not to have a mechanism for compensating for this. NACRO teams in this area, particularly draughtproofing, often make four or more journeys a day. Moreover, parent organizations may not make allowances for the poor infrastructure of mid-Wales when evaluating efficiency.

Unlike Victim Support in mid-Wales, which can interact with other voluntary bodies in the area which offer help in a related way, NACRO may possibly have suffered from a lack of contact with relevant agencies. A lot of time was expended upon maintaining a 'quota' of ex-offenders, resulting in a heavy dependence on the probation service. In areas where there is a prison located, schemes were able to visit and 'sell' the CP and also to gain a greater insight into the work of another branch of NACRO, the Prisons Link Unit. Prison visits from mid-Wales schemes were infrequent, and the physical isolation of the area limited the amount of input from more specialist staff. This was alleviated to some extent by the activities of regional staff who visited on a regular basis, but NACRO had to dispense with the services of most of them shortly after the start of Employment Training. ET brought about a network of agencies involved in the programme, with regular meetings designed to promote interaction and uniformity of provision, but as all of these were general training organizations, it was of little use to an organization with a large proportion of the disadvantaged. ET merely increased a sense of isolation, with unfortunate repercussions for offenders.

The CP was closed in September 1988, along with the much smaller Voluntary Projects Programme, and Employment Training was the widely publicized alternative. With its promise of quality training, tailored to the needs of each individual trainee, it could have been at least a partial answer to the economic problems of the disadvantaged. Although the notion of a 'wage' for trainees was discounted by the Training Agency, a programme of well funded 'quality' training may have overcome the understandable reservations of critics of the 'training allowance' element. There were positive principles incorporated into ET: agencies participating in the new scheme had to work towards adopting an equal opportunities policy in order to qualify as bona fide training managers; and the Training Agency (formerly the MSC), appeared to recognize that less fortunate sections of the population, including offenders, warranted special attention. It produced its own literature on the employment difficulties of these people and sponsored others to do likewise, including NACRO (NACRO 1989b).

The reality, though, was that market-led Employment Training was run from its inception on a much tighter budget and with more rigorous controls than previous schemes. By the spring of 1990 the Employment Secretary had announced cuts of £350 million in the budgets of YTS and ET, against the wishes of the employer-dominated Training and Enterprise Councils (TECs) which were about to acquire responsibility for the local planning and delivery of the programme (*Guardian*, 23 March 1990). The Employment Secretary cited demographic changes in the labour market and a decline in the number of school leavers as reasons for the cuts. Employers on the TECs seemed less than enthusiastic at the suggestion that private companies should fund more training in return for tax concessions. Employment Training now looked far less compatible with the needs of the underprivileged, and less likely to promote good-quality training. NACRO was among the first of the sponsoring agencies to suffer the consequences.

A first wave of closures occurred within seven months of the start of ET. Rural centres were small and particularly vulnerable. Falling unemployment in Powys and the difficulty of attracting people to ET ensured that NACRO's employment training centre in that county was one of the first to close. The organization's status as a specialist agency for the disadvantaged was insufficient protection for these centres. Furthermore, NACRO's reputation of being 'close to government to say the least' (Ryan 1983, 140) obviously extends only to its relationship with the Home Office, benefiting its more prestigious crime prevention schemes, and not to the quangos which run Employment Training. Aberystwyth was amalgamated with the NACRO centre at Milford Haven, but enlarging the unit failed to strengthen it and another funding crisis forced its closure in

December 1990. By the spring of 1991, all the staff of NACRO's training centres in Gwynedd were facing redundancy.

Future Prospects for Victims and for Offenders

In the area under examination in this study, Victim Support would appear to be going from strength to strength. In terms of national guidelines for the running of a scheme, North Powys Victim Support looks exemplary. Government funding has secured the services of a full-time co-ordinator, who provides an overview of the philosophy and practice of the service, allocates resources and has overcome many past criticisms of victim support. Such good practice will hopefully be translated to Dyfed when the new scheme becomes fully operational.

It is possible, of course, that central funding will cease at some future point, owing to a change in government priorities. But as each victim survey or set of crime statistics is published, so the public profile of the needs of victims is raised. For some years after its inauguration, Victim Support found that drawing the attention of the public was not as easy as might have been imagined, but it has now started to seep into the national consciousness as a 'worthy' cause. As things stand, it would be a foolish or insensitive government that withdraws support totally. Even if such an eventuality were to occur, Victim Support schemes have a far greater autonomy than NACRO schemes have ever enjoyed. For the latter, a decision taken further up the hierarchy is final; for a Victim Support scheme its volunteer composition may be its power base. When a NACRO scheme is closed, its staff disperses in order to find alternative employment. If a Victim Support scheme were to have its funding withdrawn, it would find difficulty in continuing although, with the volunteers remaining, the possibility exists for the maintenance of a limited service. Victim Support, through necessity, has sustained a tradition of local fund-raising, which presents a potential for expanding these funds. The resultant service would most likely be far inferior to the present arrangements, but nevertheless some form of service could perhaps be preserved.

NACRO has always been heavily dependent upon central and local government funding. The money it receives from other sources, usually charitable trusts, represents a far smaller part of its income.[5]

[5] NACRO New Careers Training received £42,514,204 from the Training Agency for the year ended 31 March 1990, and £668,466 from other sources (report of the council and accounts). NACRO Community Enterprises Ltd and the National Association for the Care and Resettlement of Offenders are audited separately. Their incomes are far smaller than NCT, but similarly they receive the bulk of their incomes from central and local government.

Employment Training was meant to afford greater opportunity for the generation of locally raised income, but this presumed a popularity for the programme which failed to materialize. The exigencies of state funding often leave little room for manœuvre, and then priorities have to be reassessed. Initiatives in rural areas, made vulnerable by their smallness of scale, are more likely to undergo curtailment and face cessation. In some spheres of activity, alternatives may exist but in mid-Wales there were no non-statutory bodies to replace NACRO, and there are none on the horizon.

So, ironically, while Victim Support thrives, the organization from which it grew, NACRO, has ceased to operate in mid-Wales, and is in decline in the rest of the country. But just as there are victims in need of support here, so there are offenders. This area may enjoy a lower crime rate, but the same range of crimes occurs. Offenders here also steal cars, burgle homes, assault, rape, abuse children, rob and intimidate the elderly and even commit murder. Criminologists seem unable to satisfy themselves that there exists a causal link between unemployment and crime, but neither are they able to disprove the relationship. Meanwhile the boredom and frustration of unemployment have become a part of rural life.

What is the future for the provision of assistance to offenders? Currently all NACRO Employment Training centres in Wales are threatened with closure with the possible exception of two or three in the south and north-east. Without a change in funding priorities the likelihood is that most will collapse, leaving NACRO in Wales represented by a juvenile crime unit in the valleys and one hostel in Cardiff. The organization has always preferred the concept of 'general' provision for offenders to a specialist, sheltered workshop type of activity (Crow *et al.* 1989). Employment Training may, however, have proved that NACRO just does not have the flexibility to compete when faced with other 'general' providers of employment and training opportunities. If competition does result in the closure of NACRO centres, there are no guarantees that offenders and other disadvantaged people are going to be nurtured by these other agencies.

A small survey of NACRO ET staff in Wales,[6] who had previously

[6] Of the fifty-two NACRO staff in Wales who replied to a questionnaire issued in July 1990, thirty-five had previously worked for NACRO in the Community Programme. Of these, thirteen felt that the needs of offenders are less well catered for in ET than they were in CP, eight felt that they are better catered for, and eleven believed them to be equally well catered for. Three expressed no opinion. Of the fifty-two staff, forty-two had received no training in working with offenders. Eighteen of the forty-two worked for NACRO for more than two years, nine for more than four years. Replies were received from all staff grades (L. Hurley, unpublished survey of NACRO in Wales, 1990).

worked in the Community Programme, reveals that one-third think that the needs of offenders are now less well catered for than during CP. They tend to cite 'lack of time' as the primary reason for this, because of the pressures and increased workload of Employment Training. It is possible, though, that general provision will inevitably attract staff who are interested in working with the disadvantaged as a whole and not specifically concerned to work with offenders.

Training staff to identify and accommodate the needs of offenders is one way of inducing a greater concern for their welfare, but the same survey reveals that three-quarters of those who responded had received no training whatsoever in working with this group. One-third of these staff had worked for NACRO for more than two years; one-sixth had worked for NACRO for more than four years. There is no suggestion that a lack of formal training entails a lack of concern, but failure to train may indicate a breakdown in the mechanism which ensures a measure of control over the quality of service. Perhaps offenders were moving to the periphery, not just in ET but in the CP as well. Perhaps they deserve better treatment, for all our sakes. And perhaps it is time for NACRO to reconsider its strategy for areas like mid-Wales and reopen the debate about 'general provision' versus 'specific'. A service for offenders which guarantees quality may, ultimately, be more important than one which promises them anonymity.

Any reluctance by offenders to associate with NACRO might be overcome by the establishment of small-scale, intensive projects existing specifically to train offenders in skills which are both commensurate with their capabilities and attuned to the requirements of their localities. Even in areas of high unemployment this might be just enough to ensure meaningful employment rather than a life on the dole interspersed with brief periods on whichever programmes are fashionable at the time. As to the cost, it is doubtful that the Department of Employment would become involved. But is it beyond the capacity of NACRO to connect with other sources of funding by emphasizing the significance of the issue of unemployment in the fight against crime, even in areas like this?

Bibliography

Box, S. (1987) *Recession, Crime and Punishment* (London, 1987).

Brenton, M. (1985) *The Voluntary Sector in British Social Services* (London, 1985).

Christie, N. (1986) 'The ideal victim' in E. A. Fattah (ed.), *From Crime Policy to Victim Policy* (London, 1986).

Clarke, R., Ekblom, P., Hough, M. and Mayhew, P. (1985) 'Elderly victims of crime and exposure to risk', *Howard Journal*, 24 (1985), 1–9.

Corbett, C. and Maguire, M. (1988). 'The value and limitations of victim support schemes', in M. Maguire and J. Pointing (eds.), *Victims of Crime* (Milton Keynes, 1988).

Crow, I., Richardson, P., Riddington, C. and Simon, F.(1989) *Unemployment, Crime and Offenders* (London, 1989).

Fattah, E. A. (1989) 'Victims and victimology: the facts and the rhetoric', *International Review of Victimology*, 1 (1989), 43–66.

Finegold, D. and Soskice, D. (1988) 'The failure of training in Britain: analysis and prescription', *Oxford Review of Economic Policy*, 4, 3 (1988), 21–53.

Gill, M. L. and Mawby, R. I. (1990) *Volunteers in the Criminal Justice System* (Milton Keynes, 1990).

Hatch, S. (1980) *Outside the State* (London, 1980).

Hodgkin, N. (1971) 'The New Careers project at Vacaville: a Californian experiment', *Howard Journal of Penology and Crime Prevention*, 13 (1971), 184–211.

Holtom, C., and Raynor, P. (1988) 'Origins of victim support philosophy and practice', in M. Maguire and J. Pointing (eds.), *Victims of Crime* (Milton Keynes, 1988).

Maguire, M. (1982) *Burglary in a Dwelling* (London, 1982).

Maguire, M. and Corbett, C. (1987) *The Effects of Crime and the Work of Victim Support Schemes* (Aldershot, 1987).

Mawby, R. I. and Gill M. L. (1987) *Crime Victims: Needs, Services and the Voluntary Sector* (London, 1987).

Maxfield, M. (1984) *Fear of Crime in England and Wales* (London, (HORS no. 78), 1984).

Mayhew, P., Elliott D. and Dowds, L. (1989) *The 1988 British Crime Survey* (London, 1989).

NACRO (1967) *Annual Report, 1967* (London, 1967).

NACRO (1981) *A Chance to Learn* (London, 1981).

NACRO (1983) *Annual Report, 1982–3* (London, 1983).

NACRO (1986) *Annual Report, 1985–6* (London, 1986).

NACRO (1988) *Annual Report, 1987–8* (London, 1988).

NACRO (1989a) *Education and Training for Offenders* (London, 1989).

NACRO (1989b) *Employment and Training for Disadvantaged People in the 1990s* (London, 1989).

NAVSS (1990) *Annual Report, 1989/90* (London, 1990).

NAVSS (undated) *Briefing Paper* (London).

Newburn, T. and Merry, S. (1990) *Keeping in Touch: Police–Victim Communication in Two Areas* (London, 1990).

Normandeau, A. (1989) 'For a charter of rights for crime victims', in E. A. Fattah (ed.), *The Plight of Crime Victims in Modern Society* (London, 1989).

Pearl, A. and Reissman, F. (1965) *New Careers for the Poor: The Non-Professional in Human Service* (New York, 1965).

Rock, P. (1990) *Helping Victims of Crime* (Oxford, 1990).

Ryan, M. (1983) *The Politics of Penal Reform* (London, 1983).
Shapland, J., Willmore, J.and Duff, P. (1985) *Victims in the Criminal Justice System* (Aldershot, 1985).
Soothill, K. and Holmes, J. (1981) 'Finding employment for ex-prisoners: a ten-year follow-up study', *Howard Journal of Penology and Crime Prevention*, 20 (1981), 29–36.
Zander, M. (1975) *Diversion from Criminal Justice in an English Context* (Chichester, 1975).

8

Community Care: the law and rural areas

JOHN WILLIAMS

Introduction

This chapter will examine some of the practical implications surrounding the implementation of recent social services legislation in sparsely populated rural areas. It is not an empirical study. Instead it considers the extent to which the principal social services legislation enables service providers to take into consideration the special components which feature in such areas and which are not characteristics of areas of relatively high population density. The debate on the relative benefits of 'town' versus 'country' living is not an issue in this essay. Instead, it discusses some of the practical effects of identifiable differences. Some research has concluded that the perceived advantages and disadvantages of town and country (or urban and rural) living are not as great as may be claimed.[1] However, whatever variety may or may not exist between the quality of services in these two types of area, there are practical differences in the method by which social, health and related services are to be delivered.

There is some difficulty in defining what is meant by 'rural'. To some extent the definition is highly subjective. Thus some may describe as rural an area that others would regard as urban. For example, the inhabitants of Little Baddow in Essex might regard themselves as rural dwellers. However, the inhabitants of

[1] See for example Gordon Grant, 'The rural–urban dichotomy in social care: rhetoric and reality', in Joyce Lishman (ed.), *Social Work in Rural and Urban Areas* (Aberdeen, 1984), 46–8.

Y Gors in Dyfed would consider themselves rural and the people of Little Baddow as urban dwellers. Within their own terms of reference both are probably correct. Of more significance than individual perceptions are matters such as communications, size and distribution of the population, and distance travelled to a principal centre of population. These are the factors which present service planners with problems.

For the purposes of this essay, 'rural' will refer to remote sparsely populated areas where communications are poor: 'urban' will refer to areas of relatively dense population having good communications. The following table illustrates the wide divergence of population distribution between different counties in England and Wales.[2]

Table 8.1

County	Pop. (1000s)	Area (sq. km)	Persons per sq. km
Tyne and Wear	1130.5	540	2093.6
South Glamorgan	403.4	417	969.6
Surrey	999.8	1679	595.4
Shropshire	400.8	3490	114.8
Dyfed	348.4	57771	60.4
Northumbria	301.4	5032	59.9

The figures in table 8.1 are somewhat misleading if they suggest that counties are wholly rural or wholly urban. For example, within Dyfed there is a marked difference between the density of the population within the districts that make up the county.[3]

Table 8.2

District	Pop. (1000s)	Area (sq. km)	Persons per sq. km
Carmarthen	55.8	1180	47
Ceredigion	67.0	1794	37
Dinefwr	38.9	977	40
Llanelli	74.1	233	318
Preseli	70.7	436	62
South Pembs.	41.9	438	96

Such diversity requires service providers to plan and implement for an urban area with a high density of population (Llanelli at 318

[2] *Regional Trends*, 25 (1990).
[3] Ibid.

persons per square km is just below the average for England), and for areas such as Ceredigion at 37 people per square km.

Rural Life

'Traditional rural life'

A Gallup public opinion poll conducted in 1939 asked: 'If you were in a position to live where you liked would you choose the city or the country?' Not surprisingly 61 per cent of those asked elected for the country and 39 per cent for the city.[4] Attitudes do not appear to have changed. The drift from town to country, particularly by retired people, indicates the desire to retreat from the pressures caused by urban life. However, assumptions are made about the quality of rural life that may not always be correct. Many of them stress the closeness of rural communities and the mutual support and benefits that flow from it. The belief that God made the country and people made the towns still prevails.[5] However, the view of the country gleaned on a holiday visit is far removed from the reality of rural living.

The perceived traditional strength of rural communities as direct providers of community care depended upon their being relatively self-contained economic and social units. A typical rural community would consist of its own school, church and/or chapel, shop, post office and public house. The local economy was based primarily upon agriculture. Not only would it be the main direct employer, it would also provide indirect employment, blacksmiths, agricultural engineers, hauliers and dairies being the main examples. Two important consequences flowed from this. Firstly, young people tended to stay within the rural community as it provided employment. Very often young people continued to live in the family home. As their parents grew older they would provide necessary care and support. Secondly, social intercourse was an inevitable consequence of rural living. People met at church or chapel; children attended the same local school; the shop, post office and blacksmith were regular meeting places. In this environment it was difficult to feel isolated. A word of caution must, however, be sounded. It is too easy to idealize this 'traditional' cosy view of rural life and to ignore the reality of change and instability which have been features of rural history. When answering a question such as that posed by Gallup, we refer to the romanticized view of rural life and tend

[4] George H. Gallup, *The Gallup International Public Opinion Polls – Great Britain 1937–75*, vol. 1 (New York, 1976).

[5] See William Cowper, *The Task* (1st edn., London, J. Johnson, 1795.

to ignore the realities. It was a harsh and often cruel environment where exploitation and poverty prevailed. Nevertheless many of those features so conducive to community care were present even though we today tend to consider them in isolation rather than in a proper historical setting.

The decline of 'traditional' rural communities

Recent years have witnessed a decline in the economic and social structure of traditional rural communities. One significant contributory factor has been the reduction in direct and indirect employment in agriculture. The figures in table 8.3 illustrate the decline in direct employment in agriculture from 1971 to 1988.[6]

Table 8.3

1971	1979	1981	1983	1986	1988	1989
450	380	363	350	329	313	300

(figures in thousands)

A decline has also occurred in the number of self-employed people within the agricultural industry (see table 8.4).

Table 8.4

1971	1979	1981	1983	1986	1988	1989
314	286	276	272	274	268	267

(figures in thousands)

This lost employment has been replaced partly by part-time or casual employment. Tourism has replaced some of the jobs lost in agriculture, although this tends to be seasonal work.

The decline of the traditional rural economy has had an impact on the social fabric of rural communities. Rural life is perceived as being tranquil and as embodying the community spirit lost in the urban communities. These assumptions must be challenged, and it is important that they do not become built into the planning of community care services. One supposition made is that rural communities are more caring. However, this presupposes that the features of rural life that once provided a framework for such caring still exist. A number of factors have conspired to destroy that structure. Rural shops, once the focal points of community life, have closed. They are unable to compete with the large

[6] *Social Trends*, 21 (1991).

urban-based superstores. Many rural post offices have disappeared. Whereas these closures do not affect the car owner, they do have dire consequences for elderly people or young families who may have relied on them. Not only are they denied the service, but they are also made to feel isolated in their own communities. Such facilities performed not only an economic function but a social one as well. The decline of the local church and chapel have added to this feeling. These institutions were providers of informal social care and helped prevent a feeling of isolation. Many churches and chapels have closed and been sold, very often for conversion to luxury housing sold to incomers. Others have remained open but now share a minister with a number of other churches. Again, this adds to a feeling of isolation if visits from a minister are more infrequent and locally held services held one Sunday in four.

Another myth is that children in rural areas enjoy a much better quality of life than their urban-based counterparts. The closure of rural schools on supposed economic grounds has resulted in children being bused to larger schools in nearby centres of population. Rural schools provided a meeting point for children both during school hours and when engaged in after-school activities such as sports and the performing arts. It was an important part of their development that they mixed with other children from their own immediate community. Similarly parents felt a part of the rural school. It was a focal point for a wide range of activity. The closure policy has meant that children now leave their own community early in the morning and have to endure a bus ride to a large town-based school. They may establish friendships with other children at the school. However, these may be difficult to pursue outside the confines of the school owing to transport problems. Children may feel isolated in their own communities. The alternative community offered to them is one that lasts no longer than school hours.

An inadequate supply of low-cost housing has contributed to the social decline of rural areas. Partly this is a consequence of the selling-off of the public sector housing stock and the restrictions preventing local authorities from reinvesting the proceeds of sales in new public sector provision. Planning control has also contributed to a reduction in the rural housing stock. Low wages in rural areas create a demand for rented accommodation, yet very often such accommodation is no longer available. The traditional tied cottage has disappeared along with agricultural jobs. Unfortunately the vacated properties are invariably priced beyond the means of people living within the community. Farmers have seized the opportunity to acquire much-needed capital by selling the properties to incoming people with the necessary money. Watkin and Winter in their study in West Devon, Boothferry and the Cotswolds concluded that rural dwellers rarely benefit from such conversions.[7] Alternatively, former tied housing has been used for holiday accommodation which is often left vacant for a significant part of the year. Thus unemployment in agriculture provides a double blow by depriving the community of both jobs and housing.

The deregulation of public transport has in many respects compounded the decline of the rural community. If services are no longer available in the immediate community, mobility becomes increasingly important. Gant and Smith concluded that.

> (N)otwithstanding the stability of the bus service since deregulation, the legislation has created serious consequences for the car-less elderly in the smaller and less accessible settlements that have already lost their basic services.[8]

They found that the network and frequency of services in the north Cotswolds has suffered since deregulation. Small bus companies are no longer able to cross-subsidize their routes. Car-sharing schemes and village community bus schemes have mitigated some of the effects of deregulation. However, the absence of a reliable public transport system for rural communities has confirmed the view that rural life now has much more to offer the car-owning commuter.

Recent Developments in Social Services Law

Social services law has undergone a radical change in recent years. Two pieces of legislation are primarily responsible for these developments; they are the Children Act 1989 (1989 Act) and the National Health Service and Community Care Act 1990 (1990 Act). The 1989 Act came fully into force in October 1991; the community care part of the 1990 Act was fully implemented in April 1993. Both pieces of legislation share common philosophies. They are both based upon the idea that living in the community is invariably better for people who may have social welfare needs than living in an institution. Community living improves the quality of life of adults and children. However, the two Acts recognize that a prerequisite of community living for such people is the provision of community-based services designed to maximize the 'normality'

[7] C. Watkins and M. Winter, *Superb Conversions* (London, 1988).

[8] R. L. Gant and J. A. Smith, 'The elderly and disabled in rural areas: travel patterns in the north Cotswolds', in T. Champion and C. Watkins (eds.), *People in the Countryside: Studies of Social Change in Rural Britain* (London, 1991), 121. See also R. L. Gant and J. A. Smith, 'Cotswold buses: endangered species?', *Buses*, 37 (1985), 58–61.

of the person's life. For example, an adult with a physical disability living in the community may require services such as meals on wheels, home help, transport and home adaptations if he or she is to enjoy to the full the benefits of the community. A child with learning disability may require special educational provision and the opportunity to participate in recreational activities. Informal carers will also require assistance. In the past the informal carers' interests have been neglected. It is crucial that they receive assistance through the giving of advice and practical support such as respite care.

The 1990 Act is largely based on the recommendations made by Sir Roy Griffiths in his report *Community Care: Agenda for Action*.[9] This report highlighted many of the defects in the law relating to the provision of community care for adults. It was set against a background of a considerable increase in the number of elderly people and people with disabilities being placed into private residential care homes or nursing homes. Very often people were placed into residential care without being assessed as requiring it. This practice was encouraged by the funding arrangement whereby payment would be met by the Department of Social Security. The changes in the 1990 Act are intended, in the words of the government White Paper, to 'enable people to live as normal a life as possible in their own homes or in a homely environment in the local community'.[10] Statutory agencies, private enterprise and the voluntary organizations must provide the right amount of care and support to help people achieve maximum possible independence and achieve their full potential. The White Paper also recognizes the importance of giving people a greater say in how they live their lives and the services they need to help them do so. Promoting choice and independence underlies the philosophy of the legislation. Four key components of community care are identified:

services that respond flexibly to the needs of individuals and their carers;
services that allow a range of options for consumers;
services that intervene no more than is necessary to foster independence;
services that concentrate on those with the greatest need.

The role of the social services in the provision of community care services will change from that of near-monopoly supplier to that of an enabler. Local authorities will be required to purchase

[9] London, 1987.

[10] *Caring for People: Community Care in the Next Decade and Beyond*, Cm 849 (London, 1990), para. 1.8.

care services from the for-profit sector and from the voluntary organization. A rapid growth in the number of non-statutory providers is a central element in the thinking behind the changes. This growth is essential to maximize the choice available to service users. Local authorities will be committed to reducing their role as direct providers. How they intend to achieve this will have to be spelt out in their community care plans.

The 1989 Act imposes a general duty on local authority social services departments to

> (a) safeguard and promote the welfare of children within their area who are in need; and (b) so far as is consistent with that duty, to promote the upbringing of such children by their families by providing a range and level of services appropriate to those children's needs.[11]

Thus, where consistent with the child's welfare, social services are under a general duty to provide services to keep the family together rather than allow the child to be placed in accommodation or taken into care. Local authorities must facilitate the provision of services by voluntary organizations, and they may make arrangements for services to be provided by the for-profit sector.[12] This duty is owed to 'children in need'. A wide definition of children in need is found in s. 17(10). Under this section a child shall be taken to be in need if

> (a) he is unlikely to achieve or maintain, or to have the opportunity of achieving or maintaining, a reasonable standard of health or development without the provision for him of services by a local authority under this Part; (b) his health or development is likely to be significantly impaired, or further impaired, without the provision for him of such services; or (c) he is disabled.

This is a deliberately wide definition which gives individual local authorities the opportunity of responding to their own social and physical environment. One factor which is relevant in rural areas is that of rural isolation. A child living in a remote rural area, with little opportunity to meet other children or be involved in groups and societies, may be unlikely to achieve or maintain a reasonable standard of development. Closure of rural schools and the need for more services such as mobile libraries increases that feeling of isolation. This feeling may be even greater if the child has a physical or mental disability. Parents may also feel isolated and abandoned.

[11] S. 17(1), Children Act 1989.
[12] Ibid., s. 17(5).

Both pieces of legislation present many challenges to local authority social services departments and to other statutory agencies such as health, education and housing. The transition from the role of the near-monopoly supplier to that of services purchaser requires a radical reorganization of social services departments. The greater emphasis on inspection, registration and complaint is expected to lead to significant improvements in quality. Service users and informal carers will have to be integrated into the planning of services both at the individual level and also at the general planning level. All social services departments are required to address these issues. However, for local social services authorities in rural areas implementation imposes additional problems. The 1989 and 1990 Acts are primarily based on an urban community model. Built into the legislation are assumptions as to ease of communications, the existence of large centres of population, potential for maximizing use of resources such as purpose-built community centres, and the ability to introduce greater choice by developing a flourishing independent sector. Added to this are the now outdated assumptions made as to the values of rural living. What special issues face social services in rural areas when implementing this legislation? To what extent can they adapt this urban-centred legislation to suit rural needs?

Special Issues Facing Rural Areas when Implementing Community Care

What is a community?

The expression 'community care' has many different meanings. It may refer to care other than that provided within institutions such as hospitals, nursing homes, mental nursing homes or in residential care. Thus any provision of care outside such institutions will be considered community care regardless of where it is provided. This definition represents a minimalist approach to community care. It is couched in negative terms – community care is something that is not institutional care. What is required is a definition that stresses the positive side of community care and identifies clear duties for statutory agencies.

Much depends upon how the word 'community' is defined. A community can be defined in very broad terms, for example the international community. However, in the context of community care 'community' should refer to the individual's immediate environment. When considering the needs of young children, the community should normally be within 'pram-pushing distance'. Day care services should be available within the child's own immediate community rather than in a large centre of population some distance away. For the older person, community-based health services should be available in his or her own village. Branch surgeries and home visit services are required. People with disabilities are entitled to services in the vicinity of their own homes rather than many miles away. This has implications for the development of community care services in a rural area. Not all services can, or indeed should, be provided in the immediate community. There may be much to be gained from enabling rural users to take advantage of services available in large towns. However, centralizing service provision must not become an objective in itself, in spite of greater economies of scale. A highly centralized service results in users spending large parts of their day travelling. If a bus has to pick up people from a large rural area it may result in them spending many hours in uncomfortable conditions. This may be especially traumatic for people with physical disabilities. Younger children may become restless and distressed. In addition, centralized services result in people losing contact with, and ceasing to be involved in, their own home community. Therefore, service providers must ensure that there is a right balance between provision made at centralized points and services provided in the immediate rural community. Local initiatives must be nurtured, and local resources such as village halls utilized. One consequence of the closure of rural schools and places of worship is the loss of facilities that could be used as community centres. Services must, wherever appropriate, be taken to the individual's community rather than the individual to services provided in somebody else's community.

We can also take the definition of community care a little further. The traditional distinction between residential and community care is increasingly meaningless. One of the principles laid down in the Wagner Report[13] stressed the importance of the distinction between the need for accommodation and the need for service. It stated that

> People who move into a residential establishment should continue to have access to the full range of community support services. Residents should have access to leisure, education, recreational and other facilities offered by the local community and the right to invite and receive relatives and friends as they choose.[14]

Thus when people are placed into residential care it is important that they do not lose contact with their own community, even though the prospects of them returning to independent living may be very remote. If the residential care is not in the person's immediate community,

[13] Gillian Wagner, *Residential Care: A Positive Choice* (London, 1988).
[14] Ibid., 114.

provision should be made to enable the person to maintain contact with that community. When providing accommodation for a child whom it is looking after, the local authority must ensure that it is reasonably near the child's home.[15] This has implications for the provision of foster-parents in rural areas. In recruiting foster-parents, authorities must seek to achieve a fair geographical spread over a large rural area. This also applies to the provision of children's homes.

The independent sector

Central to the success of the legislation is the development of a strong independent sector. This, it is argued, will increase real choice by making available a wider range of community care services. The independent sector consists of commercial undertakings and the voluntary organizations. At present a significant proportion of residential care is provided by private residential care homes, nursing homes and mental nursing homes. With the emphasis now placed on community-based care, such private undertakings will be required to diversify the services they make available. The private sector will need to be involved in the provision of home-based services, day care facilities and other services in the community. To what extent will it be possible to achieve diversification within the private sector, given the economic disadvantages of operating within a rural area? Residential care has the advantage that the user is brought to the service. A rural location for a residential home is ideal, and some larger properties may be purchased at competitive prices. Operating costs may also be lower. However, these advantages dissipate when the provider is required to take services to the user. The cost of travel and higher staffing ratios necessary to cover sparsely populated rural areas make urban areas more attractive to the private sector. There must be doubt whether rural authorities will be able to attract the private sector, and if they do, whether it will be in sufficient numbers to produce the desired competitive edge. This latter point is particularly important, as it would be unacceptable to replace a public monopoly supplier with a private monopoly supplier.

Voluntary organizations are highly experienced in the provision of community care. They are responsible for providing a wide range of services. The Women's Royal Voluntary Service, often at the request of social services, provides meals on wheels, books on wheels, luncheon clubs and shopping trips for the housebound. Attendant schemes such as Crossroads provide essential

[15] S. 23(7) Children Act 1989. This is subject to the proviso that it is consistent with the child's welfare.

support for informal carers. The British Red Cross provides many services including escort services, holidays and the organization of clubs and societies. In addition, there are a number of support groups such as stroke clubs, Age Concern, cardiac support groups and diabetic groups. Citizens' Advice Bureaux also provide a comprehensive advice service covering housing, benefits, grants and advocacy.[16] For children there are many voluntary organizations responsible for providing day care activities such as clubs and societies. However, the increased contribution envisaged under the legislation places extra burdens on fund-raisers and organizers. Voluntary organizations are having to compete for scarce resources with high-profile appeals such as those for essential hospital equipment. These problems face voluntary organizations operating in both urban and rural areas. However, additional problems face voluntary organizations in rural areas. As with statutory agencies, voluntary organizations have to meet further costs when providing services in rural areas.

Difficulties are experienced in recruiting sufficient volunteers to cover rural areas. Volunteers may be unwilling to travel long distances, and unable to devote complete days to voluntary work. Within an urban area a half-day involvement is more feasible – there is a larger pool of potential volunteers available. Wherever possible, volunteers should be recruited on a community basis rather than from outside. However, many of the volunteers in rural communities are older people, and concern is expressed as to who will assume the responsibility when they decide to retire. Hurley in her essay notes that this has also been a problem for Victim Support Schemes.[17] The new structure of rural living has resulted in less commitment from younger people to service to the community.

There are problems in achieving a flourishing independent sector in rural areas. If, as is likely to be the case, the for-profit sector prefers to concentrate on urban provision, there will be considerable pressure on the voluntary sector to assume an even greater role as direct provider. Local authorities are required to move away from their traditional role of near-monopoly providers, and, through contracting, to purchase community care from the independent sector. For service users in rural areas the consequence of this policy may be a narrowing of choice. Additional resources must be found to meet the extra costs which will be demanded by the

[16] See J. McAllister, *Provision and Participation: The CAB Service in Wales* (Bangor, 1988).

[17] See above, p. 107.

independent sector if it is to be enabled to provide a comprehensive rural service.

Planning service provision and the exchange of information

The 1990 Act imposes a duty on local authority social services departments to prepare community care plans.[18] These three-year plans must include detailed proposals for one year and outline proposals for the subsequent two years. They will be rolled forward on an annual basis, with a new third year added annually. A plan must assess local needs, set local objectives and priorities, state how the authority intends to move away from the role of direct provider and state how it will monitor performance. Each local authority is under a statutory duty to consult District Health Authorities and Family Health Service Authorities when preparing community care plans.[19] They are also under a duty to involve voluntary organizations.[20] Planning is also required under the 1989 Act. Each local authority must take reasonable steps to identify the extent to which there are children in need in its area. They must maintain a register of children with a disability.[21] After identifying the extent of need within its area the local authority must then 'make decisions on the priorities for services provision in their area in the context of that information and their statutory duties'.[22]

Planning requires an assessment of community needs and a decision on how, and to what extent, those needs are to be met by service providers. The National Council for Voluntary Organizations (NCVO) Community Care Project identified a number of issues that arise in the planning process in relation to rural areas.[23] The project pointed out that people in rural areas have little contact with statutory services, and therefore they do not have the opportunity to make their real needs known. It stressed the importance of developing sensitive ways of identifying rural needs, and suggested that the following approaches could be adopted:

grassroots workers reporting back to agencies identifying needs in rural communities;

[18] S. 46 National Health Service and Community Care Act 1990: see John Williams, 'Community Care Plans', *Baseline*, 46 (1991), 35–7.

[19] National Health Service and Community Care Act 1990, s. 46(2)(a) and (b).

[20] Ibid., s. 46(2)(e).

[21] Children Act 1989, Part 1, Schedule 2.

[22] Department of Health, *Family Support, Day Care and Educational Provision for Young Children* (London, 1991).

[23] H. Armstrong and C. Thompson, *Community Care in Rural Areas* (London, 1986).

workers in different agencies sharing their knowledge of local communities;
consulting and involving local communities;
keeping local communities in touch with the planning process;
decentralizing funding;
considering rural areas separately from urban areas.[24]

The above suggestions represent a framework for planning within rural areas. Grassroots workers (for example, health visitors, home helps and social workers) are often in an ideal position to identify need in the community. Within an urban area these needs may be more obvious to providers. In rural areas needs are often hidden through lack of adequate communications between users and providers.

Sharing information between agencies helps build up a composite picture of need in the community. Inter-agency work assumes an even greater importance in rural areas.[25] The long distances to be travelled between clients reduces the number of visits that individual agencies can make. It is, therefore, essential that experiences of all agencies are pooled if an accurate picture of the community's needs is to be obtained. Voluntary organizations should also be involved in sharing their experiences for the purposes of the planning process. Joint planning committees will help to ensure that resources are used to the best advantage.

Local communities must be involved in the planning process. Central providers may assume that all communities have identical needs. This is demonstrably untrue as between urban and rural communities, a point that those mixed urban and rural authorities must always bear in mind. However, there are also differences between rural areas within the same authority. Some are very remote, others have better communications. Similarly the facilities available will vary, as will the demand for services. A rural community which still has its local school and its village hall will require different services from those which lack these amenities. By consulting the local communities, and not by relying exclusively on statistical returns, providers will identify the true nature and level of need within individual communities. Involving communities in a consultative process is often fraught with difficulties, but these must be overcome. Open meetings at which local councillors and officers

[24] Ibid., para. 3.2.

[25] S. 27 Children Act 1989 imposes a duty on social services, health authorities, education authorities and housing authorities to co-operate in providing community services.

of the authority are present provide a useful forum. Encouraging the establishment of local support groups through grants and use of premises enables local needs and priorities to be placed on the planning agenda. Such groups may seek to represent the views of all potential service users, young and old, sick and healthy, carers and users. Whilst these different groups have distinct needs, they also have much in common. One common interest is that they all live in the same small, isolated community. Specialized teams for the elderly, children and people with learning difficulties run the risk of failing to recognize how services can be developed across client groups. Locally based groups can assist in identifying community needs of interest to all.

Rural communities must also be kept in touch with the developments in the planning process. Word of mouth, posters and local newspapers are not always effective means of imparting information within a rural community. Merely publishing the community care plan is an inadequate response. One solution is for agencies to identify key workers charged with the responsibility for disseminating information to particular rural areas. Greater use of information technology should be explored. Pre-recorded tapes, broadsheets delivered to the door and community messages on local radio provide opportunities to inform people of what is happening. It is essential for the success of community care that people are made to feel involved and that information gets back to them. Greater thought needs to be given to providing this information to rural communities.

One particularly radical solution mooted by the NCVO project was the idea of devolving financial responsibility to the individual communities. This is the ultimate model of community care and is worthy of consideration. Service users and informal carers would assume greater responsibility for deciding how scarce resources are to be used within the community. It would enable the money to be used in a way that is sensitive to the rural communities' needs. This approach requires a central allocation of a global sum for each community and a local mechanism for allocating at the devolved level. Herein lies the main disadvantage of the system. How should the lump sum be allocated by the centre? In making such an allocation, central providers might still ignore the special needs of rural areals. Some resources would have to be retained for those services which would have to be run on a central basis. Problems also arise in deciding how the resources are to be allocated at the devolved level. Who would be accountable? How would priorities be determined? Who would be responsible for the administration of the fund? Despite these difficulties, the idea of placing some financial responsibility at a local level could provide a means by which rural communities have services suited to their special needs.

Finally the NCVO project reminds us that providers must consider rural areas separately from urban areas. Failure to do this will result in special rural needs being ignored. The urban model cannot be imposed on rural communities in the hope that it will be appropriate. Nor is it possible merely to adapt the urban model to rural conditions. Rural services need to be planned from scratch. The type of services required and the manner in which they should be delivered differ radically as between the two types of areas. Providers must realize this and act accordingly.

Conclusion

The belated recognition that the benefits of community care can be achieved only through positive support is a welcome development. The emphasis placed on community care in the 1989 and 1990 Acts provides a statutory framework within which imaginative community care policies can be developed. It is, however, a mistake to assume that there is one model of community care applicable throughout the entire country. This approach fails to acknowledge regional variations. It also fails to acknowledge the marked differences between urban and rural areas. The need for community care services is as real in rural areas as in urban communities. The nature of the rural community has changed radically. Rural communities no longer provide the informal network of support so typical of past generations. People now look to the statutory agencies for services. The legislation fails to recognize the special features of rural life. It assumed that a uniform urban model will suffice. To compensate for this, local authority social services and the other statutory agencies must adapt this legislation as best they can to accommodate these special needs.

The provision of community care in rural areas presents many distinct challenges. At a local level these challenges must be recognized as existing. Urban-based service providers must accept that in implementing the legislation there is a rural dimension that must be catered for. Central government also has a responsibility. It can no longer impose uniform legislation on the country as a whole. Social welfare legislation must be more flexible in terms of objectives set and duties imposed. The 1989 Act goes some way towards providing such flexibility, especially through its wide definition of children in need and the duty to accommodate children near their homes. It is, however, far from perfect. The 1990 Act is much more prescriptive and, for rural communities, seems unrealistically committed to a prominent role for the independent sector.

Community care provision in rural areas cannot be a second-class service. Rural dwellers are entitled to the same choice as their urban counterparts. They are entitled to have services provided in their own community rather than in somebody else's. They are entitled to have an input in the planning process. These are legitimate expectations raised by the legislation. It will be interesting to see whether that predominantly urban-based legislation allows those expectations to be realized in practice.

Index